Angela Morris and John
Wiltshire where they run t   ...~~...~~~ business.
Nelus, the subject of this book, is Angela's great grandfather,
who was born in the village of South Marston in the same
county. Although Angela and John were born in different
parts of the country – Angela close to her roots in Swindon,
and John in Worcester – they were astounded during their
research for this book to discover that their forebears had
lived and known each other in Nelus' village in the middle
of last century, and indeed, John's namesake had actually
witnessed the marriage of one of Angela' family in 1846.

"Nelus" is the culmination of four years' research, and is their
first book. Their next book is currently being researched.

NELUS

NELUS

by

Angela Morris
&
John Keene

HAMILTON & Co. Publishers
LONDON

Paperback ISBN 1 901668 47 9

Publisher

HAMILTON & Co. Publishers
10 Stratton Street
Mayfair
London

Acknowledgements

Our thanks to the following residents of South Marston for their help in our research:

Angela & Ken Taylor, Canal Cottage – for their photo of their cottage – where Nelus was born and also later wrote his diary, and where his father and mother Ephraim and Ann lived.

The owners of Exstone Cottage – for allowing us to take a photo of their cottage where Nelus and Annie once lived.

Mrs Lorrie Jones, "Yarra Glen" – for her generous help in promoting this book.

The vicar of South Marston church – for allowing us to see the church records.

Mr Irvin Vynil, "My Home" – owner of the cottage that used to belong to Edward Head, Nelus' grandfather, and for obtaining the original deeds and Edward's will.

Mr R. Norman, Headmaster of South Marston school – for letting us use the school records.

Sarah Samsum and her family, and the regulars of the Carpenters Arms – for their help in answering our questions about the village last century.

Dave, landlord of the Carriers Arms – for his help in the promotion of the book.

Our thanks to the following museums and records offices etc. for their assistance in our research:

Major Ron Cassidy, Royal Green Jackets Museum, Peninsular Barracks, Winchester.

David Davies, Light Infantry Museum, Winchester (and Major John Skinner who referred us there).

R.M.P. Training School, Roustillon Barracks, Chichester.

Public Records Office, Ruskin Avenue, Kew, Richmond, Surrey.

MOD Army Records Centre, Bourne Avenue, Hates, Middlesex.

Pamela Coleman from Devizes Museum.

Swindon Reference Library – special thanks to Roger Treferne for his help.

Trowbridge County Records Office.

Oxford Reference Library.

The Swindon Evening Advertiser for letting us see the original newspapers.

Margaret Grant of Stratton, Swindon, and Bert Hunt of Taunton, Devon (Annie Hunt's niece and nephew) – for their memories.

To Aunt Evelyn

Contents

INTRODUCTION

Fate was to lay its hand on us on a hot summer's day in August 1994, when my father was suddenly taken into hospital whilst in the middle of clearing out and disposing of premises he owned in Berkshire, formerly used as a factory and "general storage warehouse". My partner John and I had to unexpectedly drop what we were doing, and take charge of the final clearance. My father, being one of life's great eccentrics and collectors, had accumulated a vast amount of machinery, furniture, books, cars and numerous other ephemera over the previous quarter of a century that he had owned the premises, and in so doing, had converted the officers' mess of the former wartime base of the American 101st Airborne Division into a dusty time-capsule waiting to be discovered. One wing of the building had been used as the depository for all the household contents of his parents' and grandparents' houses as they died, and this was an area that I had always avoided, whenever possible, even when working in the premises in the 1970's, as it seemed to emanate an eerie atmosphere. This was partly due to the traumatic history of the building, but mainly due to the fact that it contained my grandmother's chair, which had always been occupied by her during her lifetime as she was crippled from polio, and I quite expected to find her still sitting in it. My feelings for the room were not helped by the fact that an old brass bedstead, formerly belonging to Nelus and Annie, my great-grandparents, also lay alongside this chair, and it was in this very bed that my great-grandmother Annie had died.

Typically, just to test my nerves, it was this section of the building that needed to be checked before the final contents were taken to the skip. Purely by chance we decided to physically remove two highly rusted metal chests piled on top of one another amidst the remnants of great-Gran's bed and other furniture. There, to our amazement, was what appeared to be a large wooden chest, emblazoned with the inscription "Mr.C.Head, South Marston, Swindon, Wilts" in bold black lettering on the top, and "P &

O.Cabin" on the front. On opening the lid, we discovered it was full to the brim with old pictures, photograph albums, postcard albums, letters and other personal effects. Needless to say, this immediately went home with us and not into the skip!

This metal chest, which had been painted to look like wood and leather and had lain unopened for at least thirty years, was to take over our lives for the next three years. "Mr C. Head" was in fact my great-grandfather, Cornelius Head, whose diary of his experiences in the Boer War had already been handed down in the family, and, in fact, had been published locally in 1901. The subsequent unpacking and cataloguing of the contents of the chest, combined with hours of fascinating research, form the basis of this book. The discovery provided us with more than a passing insight not only into family history, but also into rural village life at the turn of the century, the "upstairs downstairs" life in domestic service, the Boer War with all its horrors, and the local history and character writings of the "Hammerman Poet" Alfred Williams from the village of South Marston. We could never have imagined so much could have come from the contents of an old metal chest that had lain undiscovered within the family for so many years.

With the centenary of the Boer War approaching in 1999, the temptation was to republish Nelus' diary as part of a general history of the war itself. However, on the discovery of his chest, we realised that we had a complete social history of the period encapsulated within its contents, far more than just the day-to-day account of the Boer War from his diary alone. In fact, our subsequent research showed us that Nelus was involved not only with the Boer War as we had previously assumed, but had also played a very active part in the fighting in India at the end of the nineteenth century, and also in the First World War. Today, we would consider ourselves very hard done-by if we had to live through one major war, and the thought of battling through three major conflicts as Nelus had done would be almost incomprehensible to us. But Nelus was just an ordinary person of his time, and it seems that, like many of his contemporaries, his way of getting through long periods of hardship and separation from his loved ones was through the medium of poetry, some of which we have reproduced in this book.

All this wonderful material could not go to waste, and we felt morally obliged to preserve it for posterity along with the diary itself. We have therefore tried to faithfully follow his life from his birth to his death, including an account of his ancestry back through the previous traceable seven generations. Although we have been fortunate in the amount of archive material available to us, enabling us to reconstruct Nelus' life and ancestry with such detail, we would like to emphasise that his life story could as well relate to you, the reader, substituting your own grandparents, great-grandparents or other family members in his place, if only the information had survived or been traced. This was the way of life one hundred years ago, and virtually every family had someone - a father, brother, husband or sweetheart - away at the war, each with their own tale to tell.

The same applies to the history of Nelus' birthplace, the village of South Marston described in Chapter Two, as this was a typical rural settlement of the time, and its characters and development were mirrored in thousands of similar villages across the country at the end of last century. South Marston is not even an exceptionally pretty village: it is somewhere you would drive through without a second glance, giving no hint of the many colourful characters that have acted out their lives within its cottages and lanes over the centuries and its long participation in the overall social development of the country. Like many a rural village, it has played its part in the ever-changing evolution of the countryside: the Industrial Revolution, the coming of the canal system - shortly replaced by the railway network - its involvement during the Second World War with the manufacture of Spitfires at the nearby Vickers Engineering Works, and even today, with the influx of Japanese industry in the vast car manufacturing complex of Honda on the outskirts of the village.

In researching for this book, we have become well-known figures around the village, asking unanswerable questions of anybody who would listen, whereas, even a mere generation ago, our queries would have been easily resolved by the village elders. Our research has shown us how easily history can be lost, and the importance of recording it for future generations. On the other hand, if an afterlife exists, it certainly does appear that we have been guided in our quest for information to complete this book. So many coincidences have occurred in the years that we have been writing, where facts have been presented to us out of the blue, or material that we have spent days looking for has suddenly appeared from the least likely source. It almost appears that Nelus really wants his diary republished, and has helped us along the way! There is a great sense of continuity and belonging when you discover and enter a cottage once occupied by your great-great-great grandparents, and imagine that the tree standing in the garden is the same one as they would have once seen from the very same window that you are now looking out of. The world marches on, but there is still a great feeling of timelessness in situations such as this. It's a surprise to realise from their writings that our forebears all that time ago still had the same hopes and aspirations that we have today, and that really the basics of life have not changed at all.

One tremendous stroke of luck for us in our research was the writings of the poet-author Alfred Williams, who was a contemporary to Nelus in the same village, and has provided us with some fascinating descriptions of the family, which has put "meat on the bones" of some of Nelus' forebears. We were delighted to discover the previously unpublished poem on Mark Titcombe within Williams' personal notes, and to be able to present it in this book, without which publication this gem of our social history could well have been lost forever, describing so vividly as it does life in a typical nineteenth century village. Our only regret is that we have not been able to identify a large percentage of the wonderful period photographs found in the chest, as there is no longer anyone living who could identify them; surely a salutary lesson for us all to name those family snaps for the benefit of future generations!

It is fascinating to note that a large number of the family names that were in the village one hundred years ago are still there now, or very close by in the surrounding area. The people we speak to today - their ancestors have spoken to our ancestors over countless centuries. The coincidences go on. It was discovered in the parish records at South Marston that a John Keene (my partner's namesake) had witnessed a Head family wedding with his mark in 1846; further research showed that our two families had coexisted in the same village throughout most of the nineteenth century, and this came as a complete surprise as we had been brought up in different parts of the country, and would never have dreamt of this family connection from 150 years ago.

Our legacy from this exercise has given us a new concept on life. Those that have gone before us have lived their lives, and all their worries, cares and concerns, which seemed so important to them at the time, are of no consequence any more. It is our turn at life now! Perhaps somebody in the not too far distant future may pick up this book and wonder at our lives, as we have done with Nelus' life, although in comparison our lives have been very mundane!

We can only hope that the what follows brings as much pleasure and interest to you the reader, as we have experienced in its research and writing.

Chapter One

NELUS' ANCESTRY

Cornelius Christopher Head was born in 1872 in the rural village of South Marston, near Swindon, Wiltshire, and was probably named after his paternal uncle, Cornelius, who was born in the village in 1832. Although the name Cornelius is virtually unheard of in our time, it was once quite a popular name, and frequently appears over the centuries in the parish records.

Cornelius - or Nelus as he was affectionately called - was the latest in a long line of "Heads" in the village, where the direct link of father to son can be traced back to 1734, when the first family reference appears in the parish records in the village church, recording the death of the Reverend John Head (Nelus' great, great, great grandfather) and, in the same year, the birth of his third child, Elizabeth. The family was, in fact, of good local stock, as the Reverend John was born in the neighbouring village of Stanton FitzWarren, where every generation of his forebears are listed back to 1580.

The parish of South Marston is fortunate in being one of only a handful in the County still in possession of its own registers, which date back to 1539, and record in a vast variety of scripts the "hatching, matching and dispatching" of the good people of Marston.

There are four main registers kept in the church, the oldest dating from the passing of an act of Parliament making the keeping of Parish records compulsory throughout the Country, and covering the period 1539 to 1662. The records were written in English, and not in Latin as many manuscripts of the period were, but are scarcely legible in places due to the variety of different handwriting, and the use of Old English characters. It is interesting to note that although the early registers cover some of the most

6

significant periods in our country's history, from the reign of Henry the Eighth, with the dissolution of the monasteries, right through to the defeat of the Spanish Armada, the regicide of King Charles the First, the Civil War and subsequent Restoration, no mention is made of these national events in any of these parochial records. Shakespeare, Milton, Spencer and many other great names graced this period, but rural little Marston was content to record its own concerns, and let the affairs of the rest of the world pass it by.

On examining the second register, covering the period 1662 to 1720, we will be informed from the script that this is "A true and perfect register of all ye baptisms, marriages, and buryalls in South Marston in ye County of Wiltes, began in ye yeare of our Lord God, 1662." This title was written "By Mee Hen: Dudley, Curate."

The third register, from 1721 to 1812, is "A register of all the baptisms, marriages, and buryalls in the Chappellry of South Marston in the Parish of Highworth, commencing this present year of Our Lord God 1721." This title was written by "H.Haggard, Curate". Probably the Reverend John Head, mentioned above, had a hand in some of the entries in these last two registers.

The high infant mortality rate is sadly reflected in these records, along with the occasional comment of "base born", disdainfully announcing the arrival into this world of some poor child without the benefit of a resident father. Not everybody died young, however, and some even comfortably exceeded their allotted "three score years and ten". Nelus' own grandfather, Edward, was one of these fortunates, and survived to the grand old age of 85 years before duly claiming his place in the village churchyard, six years after his beloved wife Elizabeth, and after helping to populate the village with no less than eight children, including our hero's namesake, Cornelius, and Jesse who will be referred to later.

Edward himself was from a large family, being one of nine children born to parents John, a carpenter, and Mary. He was born in September 1804, and was the middle child of nine, with five sisters and three brothers - two of them named John. The first John was born in July 1803, but only survived for less than a month. Eight years later, when John and Mary had a further son, he too was christened John, probably to perpetuate a favoured family name, and also with the high infant mortality rate at the time, it was a fairly common practice to name a subsequent child after one that had died in infancy. Edward became a shoemaker by trade, or cordwainer, as they were described in those days, as did his brother Thomas. Mary, his mother, survived his father by twenty-eight years, before dying in February 1855. We know from the South Marston Estate particulars of 1842, that Mary owned a property near to the church, called Elm Cottage, which was occupied by her sons Edward and Thomas, and their brother-in-law William Britten who had married their sister Martha on 19th October 1822. (Poor William was not very fortunate in marriage, as he was widowed from Martha in 1830, and again within a few years on the death of his second wife Hannah, whom he had married in 1831.) Mary herself was not registered as living in this cottage in the 1851 census, and had therefore probably gone to live out her widowhood away from the village, with one of her married daughters. It is likely that the cottage, which by all accounts was in a sorry state, was sold after her death in 1855 to Mr Alfred Bell, the owner of the manor and most of the village, who since purchasing the estate in 1852, had undertaken an improvement program for the whole village. This included buying the ancient tumble-down cottages from the owners who would sell, demolishing and rebuilding them, and then letting them back to the villagers on new tenancies, and although Elm Cottages was originally one dwelling, he had it rebuilt as two semi-detached houses.

Edward and Thomas must have learnt their skills from outside the family, as their father, John, held a different trade to theirs, as a carpenter, and with only two sisters and no brothers, there was no one else to teach the boys their art. They worked as the village shoemakers from their parents' cottage, as no doubt there was relatively more room to operate from there than from Edward's own cottage that he occupied with his family. The family appears to have accumulated a little wealth, for they also owned a plot of land in the village, the dimensions of which are discernible from a faint inscription in the family bible dated 1837, and amounted to 300 cubits in length and 550 cubits wide. (A cubit being an old unit of measurement, taken as the distance between the elbow and the end of the middle finger.) Edward's cottage was one of seven situated on a narrow lane called Reeds Row, now long gone, which passed to the side and rear of the church, and was demolished in 1884 in order that the churchyard could be extended. Almost certainly these cottages would have been small single storey dwellings, crudely constructed from wattle and daub, and providing the most basic of family accommodation, and it is hard to imagine now how Edward and his wife Elizabeth managed to raise all of their eight children in such cramped conditions. The village inhabitants today have no memory of this tiny road, and there is no physical trace remaining except for a stand-pump, which formerly served these simple dwellings, strangely situated amongst the tombstones in the churchyard.

South Marston churchyard showing the original stand-pump from Reeds Row still standing amongst the tombstones

In 1870, when their children had grown up, they bought a cottage on the Highworth Road into the village for the sum of sixteen pounds, with the help of a mortgage from a local gentleman, Robert Stannard Foreman. It was common practice at this time, before the appearance of building societies and the widespread usage of banks, to obtain help from the local landowner or squire to buy your cottage, often on a lifetime mortgage arrangement, where, in return for the payment of interest at around 5%, the borrowing was not repaid until the borrower died or the property was sold.

Elizabeth died at the age of 76, and was buried in the village churchyard on the 9th June 1884, the same year that her old cottage where she had raised her children was demolished to extend the churchyard. It is ironic to think that she may have been buried on the very site of her old home. Edward continued to live in their cottage after her death, and in the October of the same year, he sold part of his garden to his youngest son Jesse, the village mason, to build a house for himself and his wife Jane. From the deeds of the cottage, we see that the land was conveyed from Edward to Jesse for "the consideration of five shillings now paid by the said Jesse Head to the said Edward Head and also in consideration of the natural love and affection which the said Edward Head has for the said Jesse Head and for diverse other good causes and considerations." From documents available, it appears that Jesse had used his skills as a mason to renovate his father's cottage, and in return was given the plot of land at a nominal price to build his own house on. To this day, Edward's cottage still stands, although Jesse's has been demolished. Only the scullery remained, and that has now been incorporated into the existing building. It is interesting to note that the current building and garden incorporates the fabric and site of six original villagers' cottages.

Edward died on the 25th February 1890. It is sad to see that, although he made elaborate arrangements for the division of his estate and the provision for his widow in his will, written in 1879, by the time of his death eleven years later, his total worth was less than £5.00. At least he managed to keep out of the workhouse.

Only two of Edward's sons followed him in his trade as shoemaker - Ephraim, (Nelus' father) who was born in 1838, and Frederick who was born in 1846. Ephraim would have learned his trade working alongside his father for a while, furnishing the villagers with their footwear, and eventually, as the eldest, would have taken over "his father's patch".

Edward and Elizabeth's (Nelus' grandparents) cottage in South Marston, (brick cottage in centre with two chimneys)

The Cobbler's Bill

Here's cutting and contriving
Hammers, nails and driving
Hemp, wax, and leather;
Madam, if you please
To pay me your fees,
It's fourpence ha'penny altogether.

(From the notes of Alfred Williams)

The small village would not have had sufficient population to support a further craftsman, and therefore, having served his apprenticeship with his father, Frederick moved on to pastures new, disappearing from the parish records between 1871 and 1881. The family bible, in which was inscribed the land details already mentioned, was probably given to Ephraim on his eleventh birthday, as the only other inscription within proudly proclaims:

"Ephraim Head, his book, South Marston, Wilts, 1849."

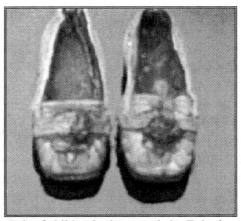

Pair of children's shoes made by Ephraim

Ephraim, as the village shoemaker, later continued to ply his father's trade from a small rented cottage on the main Shrivenham Road through the village, alongside the Wilts and Berks Canal. His house, called "Canal Cottage", still stands to this day, although it now consists of one dwelling instead of the two adjoining cottages of Ephraim's time. Sadly, the canal, once a thriving thoroughfare, has long since been infilled, but the line of its course is still discernible. Ephraim married local widow and next-door neighbour Ann Thorn in the village church on the 6th July 1867. Presumably, busy with his shoemaking he did not have much time to spread his "net" far in the search for a bride, and settled for the "girl next door", or at least "the widow next door". Had their marriage taken place two centuries earlier, they may have had to resort to a "smock wedding" as by local custom, if a man married a widow other than by smock wedding, then he took over the debts of her previous husband. Under this custom, the woman came to the man naked to show she brought with her nothing from her previous marriage, but to preserve decency she wore a smock to the wedding which her new husband had bought her. At the time of their marriage Ann already had two children, William and Olive, from her previous marriage to James Thorn, and together with Ephraim, they had three further children:

12

TO MILK IN THE VALLEY BELOW

To Milk in the Valley Below

*Obtained at Castle Eaton, and corrected at South Marston, Wilts,
where it was the favourite song of Ephraim Head, the village
shoemaker. I have not heard of the piece except about the centre
of the Upper Thames Valley.*

OH, Nancy, my heart!
    Don't you hear the sweet lark?
Don't you hear the sweet nightingale sing?
    Don't you hear the fond tale
    Of the sweet nightingale,
How she sings in the valley below?
How she sings in the valley below?

    Oh, Nancy, don't fail!
    May I carry thy pail?
May I carry thy pail to the cow?
    But the maid she replied,
    " I'll not walk by thy side,
To milk in the valley below,
To milk in the valley below."

    " Now sit yourself down
    All on this cold ground,
I'll do you no harm, I avow."
    But the more she was afraid
    For to walk by his side,
Or to milk in the valley below,
Or to milk in the valley below.

    This couple agreed,
    They were married with speed,
They were married the very next day;
    Now no more she is afraid
    To walk by his side,
Or to milk in the valley below,
Or to milk in the valley below.

Ephraim's favourite song taken from "Folk Songs of the Upper
Thames" by Alfred Williams.

Fred born in 1868; Arthur Herbert born in 1869; and Cornelius Christopher, our hero and their youngest child who was born in 1872.

Canal Cottage as it is today

Canal Cottage is today situated on the tremendously busy and noisy main road from Swindon to Oxford, and it is hard to imagine just how picturesque and peaceful it would have been when Ephraim and his family lived there a hundred and thirty years ago. The main road in front of Canal Cottage would then have been a quiet country lane, bordered by hedgerows carpeted with an abundance of colourful wild flowers and herbs, and alive with the sound of birdsong. The canal running behind the cottage would have been the busier thoroughfare, with the barges passing backwards and forwards delivering their cargoes, and passing through the locks. The waters would also have harboured a wide variety of wildlife, both above and below the surface. Although this would have appeared an idyllic scene, the close proximity of the water to the house would have created such problems as rat infestation and the need for constant vigilance over the children for fear of falling in and drowning. The proximity of the canal was a very real danger to families with children, as Henry Hawkins, the lock-keeper living in the nearby lock house discovered, for within the space of two years he lost the eldest two boys of his six children by drowning in the canal. Inside the cottage, accommodation was very cramped for a family of six, only consisting of one long, narrow, low-ceilinged room on each floor, with the upper room divided into two small bedrooms.

Richard Jefferies, another local author who lived most of his life in the nearby hamlet of Coate, gives a contemporary description of the interior of a similar cottage:

It consists of two rooms, oblong, and generally of the same size - one to live in, the other to sleep in...At one end there is a small shed for odds and ends. The shed used to be built with an oven, but now scarcely any labourers bake their own bread, but buy of the baker...The floor consists simply of the earth itself rammed down hard, or sometimes of rough pitching stones, with large interstices in between them. The furniture of this room is of the simplest description. A few chairs, a deal table, three or four shelves, and a cupboard, with a box or two in the corners, constitute the whole. The domestic utensils are equally few, and strictly utilitarian. A great pot, a kettle, a saucepan, a few plates, dishes and knives, half a dozen spoons, and that is about all. But on the mantelpiece there is nearly sure to be a few ornaments in crockery, bought from some itinerant trader.

By good fortune, a full description of Nelus' parents, Ephraim and Ann, has survived thanks to the writings of local poet and author Alfred Williams, who also came from the village of South Marston, and wrote extensively about local characters and places. Williams describes them here in an extract from his full handwritten notes which he later edited his published book "A Wiltshire Village":

THE OLD SHOEMAKER

The village shoemaker lived in the little stone cottage near the canal, and carried on the trade he had inherited from his father. Formerly he used to make many pairs of boots for the villagers, good strong substantial footwear, just the stuff for country places, and especially to wear about the farms in the wet and cold of winter, but this is at an end now. The village cobbler, at any rate, and as far as the making of new pairs of boots goes, is very nearly extinct. All the villagers now obtain their boots and shoes from the town - boots at five or six shillings a pair, shoddy cloth trousers, and jackets at a small figure; it is an age of cheapness all round. The boots are worn out in a short while, and the clothes too. A few soakings with wet betray the former; they drop all to pieces when placed before the fire to dry; and if you come into contact with the slightest projection, or strain your trousers or coat, the falsely woven fabric rips and tears, and might easily put you in a quandary. A good pair of mens' boots, made of the best leather by the village shoemaker - "Bucks", as they were called from the old fellow's nickname - cost sixteen or eighteen shillings. When we were small boys and went to school ours cost eight shillings and sixpence, as I remember, and were securely watertight. This we soon ascertained, because we made haste to try them in the first ditch or pool we came to.

The old shoemaker was of striking appearance, of fair height, and well built. His head was massive, broad forehead, heavy brows, strong fierce eyes, prominent nose, thick long hair, moustache, and abundant beard, decidedly patriarchal. To my boyish and unsophisticated mind, he seemed exactly to correspond with ideas I had conceived of the old prophets; a figure expressing dignity, gravity, profound intelligence, philosophy, and wisdom, though, of course, he did not possess these qualities, or only in a small degree. But he was shrewd enough, and grave enough, and blunt enough, with plenty of common sense, and experience of life - a hard nut to crack, argumentative, self-opinionated, outspoken and independent, agreeing well with what I have said as to original constitution of society in the village. In the spring of the year he went sheep-shearing with Dudley Sansum; these two were expert hands in cutting off the thick fleeces; they visited all the villages round about, and on the downs as well. At such times, if you wanted any repairs done to your boots, you had to take them somewhere else, to the town, or otherwise wait till a wet day came. That kept the shoemaker at home; then he set to work with hammer, awl, and wax-ends again.

His wife Ann was a kind-hearted creature, and as deaf as a post. She was as thin as a shadow, a hard worker, and a hard liver, her old face was wrinkled and brown; she had worked her fingers to the bone almost in trying to eke out enough to supplement her husband's earnings, for week in and week out his profits were very small, it was a great struggle to live. So Ann went out washing and charring and did sewing as well; from early morning till late night she was toiling and toiling to earn an honest shilling. Poor they were, and poor they were like to be: the better day did not actually dawn for them: hoping and hoping, they died before they were aware of it, in the midst of poverty, as happens to so many deluded creatures who have not the power to grasp the disposition of life, and realise the future in the present. It is always "tomorrow" "tomorrow" and "someday" with most people. With each rising of the sun it is as far away as ever, it is the present hour, the present moment that avails, we must strike at once, and put nothing off if we would do anything for our benefit. When that which we call tomorrow comes - it is only today resurrected - we shall be no better, more probably we shall be weaker and worse than before.

The shoemaker and his wife lived happily enough together, though he was often harsh and unfeeling towards her, and called her "an old fool", and shouted at her at the top of his voice, and spoke of her to everyone as "my owld ooman"; but she bore it all very patiently, and nodded and smiled, and winked now and then, and shed a few tears, and was most slavish in her attendance on him, denying herself the necessaries of life to procure things for his comfort, though she was nearly broken hearted at the end, for he fell ill with cancer, and because of her deafness would not have her at his bedside, but motioned with his arms, and told the others "to keep her away; he didn't want her there." After her husband died she continued in the cottage a little while on parish pay, and finally went to the workhouse, where she died at eighty. In her young days, as a girl, she worked about the fields for the farmer, minding the pigs and sheep, and received a piece of bacon in weekly payment. She often wept when she told you of her past experiences and had stopped and wiped the tears away with the corner of her print apron, and smiled again immediately. Then, as you turned to go, she gripped you by the shoulders and said, "Wait a minute! Now let me tell you another little bit" and went on repeating the old hardships. Laughing and crying admirably at the same time, and finally ending up with "Tis Hard for ma now, yen't" . By then, you often had the greatest difficulty to keep from bursting out into laughter in the midst of the most solemn narration. If everyone had as kind a heart as the old shoemaker's wife, how much better a great many of us would be, and the world about us as well!

As Alfred Williams mentions, Nelus' mother Ann struggled on for a while on Parish Pay of two loaves of bread a week, for a short while after Ephraim's death, but eventually ended up in the Workhouse, where she died on 28th October 1911. Their financial plight clearly shows the change in fortunes for workers at the end of the nineteenth century; Edward's estate had been split between all the children, and, for Ephraim, who followed the old village craft of shoemaker, his inheritance and the income from his business was not enough to prevent him from dying a pauper. His brother Thomas, however, prospered on the relatively high wages

Nelus' mother Ann, the Old Shoemaker's wife

from his employment in the new railway works in Swindon, and ended up owning two properties. Therefore, as far as Nelus was concerned, the family "wealth" that had been passed down over the last two centuries had now disappeared, and he was master of his own fortune. It appears strange to us that Nelus, or another member of the family, did not take Ann in, but at this time the family had become more widely dispersed, and no doubt the accommodation that most of them occupied would not have stretched to a further person in occupation. The Swindon and

Highworth Union Workhouse, situated in the village of Stratton, a matter of a mile or so across the fields from Marston, would have been her destination:

The workhouse, dingy and drab-looking, lies off the road somewhat, sixty or seventy paces. The entrance to it is barred with stout iron gates, which are generally fastened and locked, day and night as well. High elm trees overshadow the entrance, and continue in a line along the hedgerow there. Just within is the porter's lodge - a little hut big enough to contain two persons - fitted with a stove for use in cold weather; to the right and left, before the house, are some shrubs and evergreens, which look almost black from the road. On the one hand, going in, is a patch of turf with goal-posts, where the juvenile paupers forget their situation in the excitement of a game occasionally; on the other, are gardens for flowers and vegetables. Farther down on the left are outhouses and buildings where the tramps and roadsters, who are admitted for the night, pay off their score the next morning with a little healthy exercise with the saw and hatchet, or other implement. Beyond that is more ground for vegetables, worked by the permanent "staff" of the place. Here is the school 'playyard' walled round, and fenced in with iron railings like a prison; this is the shoemaker's, and there is the tailor's shop. In the front part are the master's quarters, the Board-Room, and the offices; adjoining these is the workhouse proper, where the paupers are confined. The infirmary is a new building, and is situated at the rear. The greater portion of the tragedy is here, for those detained in the other parts, though poor and unfortunate, are able-bodied enough; these are doubly wretched, in that they have no possessions of any sort, and are afflicted with diseases as well, more often of a permanent kind: there is no hope of escape for them. 'What is that man there?' I asked one old fellow, well over eighty. 'Is he going out again?' 'I dunno; I dun expect so' he replied. 'A lot as comes in stops here till they dies.' That is it precisely. The old fellow was there waiting for death to relieve him, too; but though he could see and dimly understand the fates of others he had not fully grasped the position in regard to himself. Other people's misfortunes generally strike us more forcibly than our own. There are all sorts of people in the infirmary afflicted with many and various complaints, and a few with none at all beyond that of extreme old age. Very many of them are old roadsters, who have tramped, and tramped, and tramped, until their legs were quite worn out, and they could go no farther in the journey......The other occupants of the infirmary are a miscellaneous lot. They are of all sorts, sizes, and ages. Here is a little mite of four years who fell in the fire and burned severely. He is nearly well now, and is looking bright and bonny.....In another bed, close at hand, is one very white and emaciated. He looks at me long and earnestly. Walking up to him, I recognize one I had often seen about the factory. He recognized me in return. I took him by the hand, and our eyes met. There was no need to speak; it was too evident. He was in the last stage of consumption.....Who is this pitiable looking wretch coming through the doorway here, with his head swathed in bandages, and only a part of his face visible, and even that a loathsome sore, his nose eaten away, his cheeks, too, the evil spreading all round his neck, under his chin, and everywhere? ....The man of independent spirit is deeply wounded at being brought to the workhouse; he is struck to the soul with it; it will be most likely to prove mortal.

The above is the writer Alfred Williams' description of Stratton Workhouse on visiting a friend inside.

The support of the poor has always been a problem for rural parishes, where a disproportionate number of destitute people within the parish could prove an impossible burden on the meagre resources available. The first step towards alleviating this problem was the Act of Settlement of 1662, which ensured that paupers could only receive relief from their native parishes, and this was strictly enforced throughout the eighteenth and nineteenth centuries. The passing of this Act meant freedom of movement out of their native area was only available to those who could support themselves, and anyone becoming unable to work through illness, unemployment or old age, and needing to apply for relief, was regarded as an unwelcome liability, and was referred to and often returned to the parish of their birth.

Workhouses, or poorhouses as they were sometimes known, began to be established around the 1730's, to house those in the area who could no longer support themselves, and varied in size from cottage accommodation to substantial complexes. Admission into the workhouse was the one thing that people dreaded above all else, as conditions were invariably diabolical. Once admitted, inmates were relieved of all their personal possessions, including any house or land they may own, and their own personal clothing was replaced by the "house" uniform. Men and women were strictly segregated, even married couples who had been together for many years were split up, understandably causing great distress and misery. Inmates were seldom allowed outside the premises, and visitors were few and far between; often children were even barred from playing with toys. Accommodation was often cramped, with a wide cross-section of inmates often housed together: the sane and insane, firm and infirm, the respectable craftsman and housewife fallen on hard times along with the tramp. The tramps were the one category of inmate who did tend to come and go, and may well just be admitted for the harshest part of the winter, or even just the night. They would be made to work off their keep by some menial task before departing in the morning, and those whose visits were of a regular nature were often given the job of stone-breaking for the repair of the roads. As this exercise was carried out on the roadsides, they got to hear all the local gossip, to such an extent that it became a common saying on being asked a question to which you did not know the answer: "Ask the stone-breaker!" Before entering the workhouse, the crafty tramps would hide any coins they had in their possession between the cracks in nearby walls, ready for their collection on departure.

Stratton Workhouse as it appears today, now used as a geriatric hospital.

By law, all inmates of the workhouses were required to wear a pauper's badge on their right-hand shoulder, as a mark of their status, and as a discouragement for others to join them; the badge showing a large letter "P" for pauper and a small first letter to denote their parish. The regime was harsh in the extreme, with the general reasoning that the inmates should be punished for making themselves a burden to the parish. It can therefore be understood why people would go to almost any length to stay out of "the house", and many would rather have starved to death under their own roof than suffer the ignominy of admittance to the local poorhouse. Most people desperately tried to put a little by from their meagre incomes to support themselves when they could no longer work, but there was always the danger that you would outlive your savings. The following well-known poem graphically illustrates the lack of "out relief", i.e. assistance from the Parish without admittance to the workhouse, and the hypocrisy from those responsible for the running of the establishments and the wellbeing of the inmates.

In The Workhouse

It is Christmas Day in the Workhouse
And the cold bare walls are bright
With garlands of green holly,
And the place is a pleasant sight:
For with cleaned washed hands and faces,
In a long and hungry line
The paupers sit at the tables,
For this is the hour they dine.

And the guardians and their ladies,
Although the wind is east,
Have come in their furs and wrappers,
To watch their charges feast;
To smile and be condescending,
Put pudding on pauper plates,
To be hosts at the workhouse banquet
They've paid for with the rates.

Oh, the paupers are meek and lowly
With their "Thank'ee kindly, mum's";
So long as they fill their stomachs,
What matter it whence it comes?
But one of the old men mutters,
And pushes his plate aside:
"Great God!" he cries; "But it chokes me!
For this is the day she died."

"Last winter my wife lay dying,
Starved in a filthy den;
I had never been to the parish, -
I came to the parish then.
I swallowed my pride in coming,
For, ere the ruin came,
I held up my head as a trader,
And I bore a spotless name."

"I came to the parish craving
Bread for a starving wife,
Bread for the woman who'd loved me
Through fifty years of life;
And what do you think they told me,
Mocking my awful grief?
That 'the House' was open to us,
But they wouldn't give 'out relief'.

"Then I told her 'the House' was open,
She had heard of the ways of that,
For her bloodless cheeks went crimson
And up in her rags she sat,
Crying, 'bide the Christmas here, Joe,
We've never had one apart;
I think I can bear the hunger -
The other would break my heart.'

"I rushed from the room like a madman,
And flew to the workhouse gate,
Crying, 'food for a dying woman!'
And the answer came 'too late.'
They drove me away with curses;
Then I fought with a dog in the street,
And tore from the mongrel's clutches
A crust he was trying to eat.

Back through the filthy by-lanes!
Back through the trampled slush!
Up to the crazy garret,
Wrapped in an awful hush.
My heart sank down at the threshold,
And I paused with a sudden thrill,
For there in the silv'ry moonlight
My Nance lay cold and still.

"Yes, there in a land of plenty,
Lay a loving woman dead
Cruelly starved and murdered
For a loaf of the parish bread.
At yonder gate, last Christmas,
I craved for a human life.
You, who would feed us paupers,
What of my murdered wife!

"There, get ye gone to your dinners;
Don't mind me in the least;
Think of the happy paupers
Eating your Christmas feast;
And when you recount their blessings
In your smug parochial way,
Say what you did for me, too,
Only last Christmas day."

by George R Sims

The true pathos of the last journey to the workhouse is touchingly described in "The Roadmender", (a biography by Michael Fairless, published in February 1902), in which he describes his work as a roadmender at the turn of the century, and the people and events which he encounters as he repairs the potholes on his section of a country road: an old couple's last journey together was seen and overheard by him, and he relates as follows:

There is an old couple in our village who are past work. The married daughter has made shift to take her mother and the parish half-crown, but there is neither room nor food for the father, and he must go to N----. If husband and wife went together, they would be separated at the workhouse door. The parting had to come; it came yesterday. I saw them stumbling lamely down the road on their last journey together, walking side by side without touch or speech, seeing and heeding nothing but a blank future. As they passed me the old man said gruffly, 'Tis far eno'; better be gettin back'; but the woman shook her head, and they breasted the hill together. At the top they paused, shook hands, and separated; one went on, the other turned back; and as the old woman limped blindly by I turned away, for there are sights a man dare not look upon. She passed; and I heard a child's shrill voice say, 'I come to look for you Gran'; and I thanked God that there need be no utter loneliness in the world while it holds a little child.

Nelus spent his childhood years living in his parents' cottage alongside the canal, with his older brother Arthur and his half-brother and half-sister William and Olive Thorn. His eldest brother Fred only managed to survive for two days, and was buried in the village churchyard on the 3rd of March 1868. Arthur managed to hang on to life somewhat longer, and having come within a whisper of his seventy-seventh birthday cast off this mortal coil on 2nd August 1946 due to "drowning by accidentally falling into a disused clay pit" in Cheyney Manor Road, Swindon, according to his death certificate. Memories from members of the family recount that Arthur was very partial to washing his feet whenever the fancy took him, and it is obvious that this was the cause of his downfall, as evidenced by the following contemporary report from the local newspaper:

Old Man's Death in Pool

Fell in while paddling

Last known actions of a seventy seven year old Swindon man before he met his death by drowning in Telford Pool were described by David Reddick (11) of 91 Rodbourne Road Swindon, at the inquest at Gorse Hill, on Saturday, on Arthur Herbert Head, of 19 Davis Street Swindon. The district coroner (Mr Harold Dale) returned a verdict of "Accidental Death".

He was going fishing, the boy said, when he saw the old man sitting on a seat reading a paper. When he returned, the man, who had his shoes and socks off, was standing on the steps of the landing stage on one foot, swishing his other foot in the water.

Aubrey Leslie Cornelius Head, with whom deceased lived at 19 Davis Street, said that Head had been in good health, and had no worries. "His usual practice was to have breakfast, and then go out. He had his dinner out, and came home every night at the same time for his tea. He then went out again until 10.00 p.m.

"On Thursday he went out in the morning but did not return for his tea. We thought that he might have gone to the old age pensioner's tea, but when he did not return by night, the police were informed."

About a fortnight ago, Head had a pain in the neck, and complained of dizziness, but for the last week he had been "normal for an old chap of that age".

Witness stated that he had inspected the scene of the accident. He alleged that nobody was in attendance there at the time Head fell in. Constable Truckle described how he recovered the body by dragging the pool. Doctor H. Lichtenstein said that a post mortem examination had been performed, and there was nothing to indicate that death was not by drowning.

The owner of the pool, Mr D.Horne, of Cheyney Manor Road Swindon, said that he was not at the pool because he and his wife had been to the old age pensioner's party in the Town Gardens. When he returned and viewed the pool, he saw some clothing. "I thought that the old man had gone away barefooted," explained Mr.Horne, "so I looked to see if there were any signs of a hat floating on the water. I could not see one, so I informed the police. It is a very deep pool. I am generally in attendance there myself, as people come in to swim and fish. It is the first mishap we have had for twenty seven years."

Mr Head interposed, and suggested that the question of negligence should be considered, but the Coroner disagreed, adding: "I don't know that one can say it is any more negligent of the owner than it is upon you people for allowing him to go out, and not knowing where he went." Mr Dale continued: "It is amazing what things old people will do. It was very risky for him to stand on the steps and swill his feet. Our old people will go about, and quite rightly, really otherwise their lives would be a burden."

Telford Pit in Swindon where Arthur drowned

We wondered why an old man of nearly seventy-seven should have been wandering around a "disused clay pit," but in fact, the death certificate description did not do it justice. Telford Pit still exists to this day as a charming oasis of calm within the urban development of Swindon, and is a prime example of a once popular place of recreation. It had formerly been a clay quarry for the local brick-works, and when exhausted, was filled with water to form a small lake, landscaped, and stocked with fish. It then became a popular venue for local residents to swim and fish, and it can then easily be imagined why Arthur was drawn there for a stroll on a warm August day, and where he unfortunately met his untimely death. Having spent his childhood by the canal-side, to the continuous warnings of his mother to keep away from the water, it seems ironic that drowning should have been the cause of his death in old age. We wonder if he heard the echoes of her words as he was sucked under the surface, still telling him not to play near the bank!

Arthur Herbert Head
as a young man

Nelus' half-sister Olive and
her husband Fred

Ackland Lodge, Woodstock Road, Oxford,
showing Olive and Fred in the doorway

Nelus' half-brother and half-sister were, of course, quite a bit older than him, William having been born in February 1861, and Olive in July 1863. Olive married Fred Dallaway from Oxford, and moved there with him, where they worked at Acland Hospital, which was a private nursing home, and lived in the Lodge within the grounds, fronting onto Woodstock Road. This hospital still prospers, and the external appearance of Acland Lodge is no different today than it appeared in a photograph of Olive and Fred standing by the porch one hundred years ago.

Although Nelus subsequently left South Marston, various descendants of the family have remained in evidence in the village until recent times.

Chapter Two

NELUS' BIRTHPLACE -THE VILLAGE OF SOUTH MARSTON THEN AND NOW

South Marston is an ancient village situated on the borders of Wiltshire and Oxfordshire, alongside the main Swindon to Oxford road. The name Marston, as it was commonly called by the locals last century, is of Saxon origin, and is derived from "mere stone" which meant markstone or boundry stone. Although not mentioned in the Doomsday Book, which may be a sign of independence from any feudal lord at the time, its antiquity is established by its very name and the numerous old accounts of significant Roman remains in and around the village. Sadly, there is no trace of these today, no doubt because of the effects of ploughing and quarrying for building materials, but many did survive up until the last century. Indeed, one particular site on a farm in the village was said to have encompassed an acre of land with walls up to four feet high, and was put to good use as a cattle enclosure. The old Roman road known as Ermin Street runs close by the village, and the surrounding area is well populated with Roman sites.

There would have been very little variety of employment for the people of the village up to the early part of the nineteenth century, with the standard occupation, apart from the few craftsmen, being that of agricultural labourers on the surrounding farms who worked in the very early days for little more than a piece of bacon and an occasional flagon of ale a week, progressing to very basic subsistence wages by the turn of the century. One local industry which did achieve some claim to fame for the village, and provided a degree of employment, was cheese making. North Wiltshire Cheese, as it was called, was produced in this and neighbouring villages, with most local farms having their own cheese room, and became very saleable for a long period on the London Market, providing a profitable sideline for the area, particularly with low transport costs enhanced by the new canal mentioned below. This industry is briefly described in Aubrey's "Natural History Of Wiltshire" as follows:

Now of late, sc.1680, in North Wiltshire, they have altered their fashion from thinne cheeses about an inch thick, made so for the sake of drying and quick sale, called at London Marleborough cheese, to thick ones, as the Cheshire Cheese. At Marleborough, and Tedbury, the London cheese-mongers doe keep their factors for their trade. At the end of the nineteenth century Reading was the principal seat of the London Cheese factors who visited the different farms in Wiltshire once in each year to buy the cheese, which was transported in wagons to Reading, often by circuitous routes in order to save the tolls payable on turnpike roads.

In 1804 the local economy would have been boosted by Mr James Johnson's new brickyard at Marston, to supply the construction of the new stretches of the Wilts and Berks Canal passing along the edge of the village, including four locks, two with tail bridges, and an aquaduct at Acorn Bridge, with three seven foot arches over the River Cole, which opened the following year. No doubt Marston men were employed in these works which produced 1,559,000 bricks that year, and 764,000 in 1805, and further employment would have been provided in the digging and on-going maintenance of the Canal and the manning of its locks. Records show that the annual salary of the local toll collector for the Canal Company in 1810 was £54.12.00, and the post was held by one John Theobalds. In 1842, the "wharfinger" at Marston, Mr W.Reeve, was paid £65 per annum. The canal would have become a convenient thoroughfare for the villagers after its construction, perhaps giving some their first escape from the village, but although it enjoyed a brisk period of trade from local businessmen for a while, due to various setbacks, it never really achieved any degree of financial success. From when it opened, two thirds of its traffic was on Somerset Coal, and in1837 it was also in heavy use from the Great Western Railway as a means of transport for the construction of their new railway works in Swindon, with a total of 5149 boats passing through the locks. This, however, was short lived, as the new GWR railway line from London to Bristol was opened on 30th June 1841. Running as it did, almost alongside of the canal, it very quickly took over almost all of the local traffic and started the years of decline of that form of transport. As trade usage fell, its condition deteriorated to the extent that by the early years of this century it was becoming stagnant and odorous, with its structures in a dangerous condition, and in 1906 traffic on the canal ceased altogether as parts became unnavigable. An Act in

1914 closed the canal for good, and shortly after the line of this section was completely infilled, and the four locks were finally buried in 1960. A pile of debris is all that remains of the three seven-foot arched brick aqueduct that once carried the canal over the River Cole.

Epilogue

The old canal, from bank to bank,
Is filled with reeds and rushes rank;
And down this lane of living green
March memories of what has been.

The painted barges came from town,
And busy life flowed up and down.
But there is nothing left to show
Where those old barges used to go.

Progress is always marching on;
The old canal is dead and gone,
But still we seem to hear it say,
"I, too, was Progress - yesterday."

Reginald Arkell

It is not for its history or its buildings that Marston has a claim to fame, however, but for being the birthplace and life-long home of the poet and author Alfred Williams. He was born in the village on 7th February 1877, five years after our Nelus, in Cambria Cottage, which had been built by his parents Elias and Elizabeth Williams, on a piece of land known as the "Hook", part of a meadow owned by his maternal grandfather Joshua Hughes. Alfred's father and paternal grandfather had originally come to the village from North Wales in 1852, as carpenters under the employ of the new Lord of the Manor, Mr Bell. Alfred was the fifth child of eight children, all of whom their mother struggled to bring up alone, as their father deserted them when they were young. He gained his nickname "The Hammerman Poet" from his job in the Great Western Railway works in the nearby railway town of Swindon; the awful conditions of which he so graphically described in his book "Life In A Railway Factory". He is best known for his writings on rural village life, bringing the past alive with his colourful character descriptions, including some of Nelus' own family, as we have seen with "The Old Shoemaker" in Chapter One. After marrying his childhood sweatheart Mary Peck, Alfred finally got his wish and was accepted into the Army in November 1916, despite an adverse medical history. He was posted to India and stationed at Ranikhet, a place he fell in love with; so much so, that on his discharge and return to the village after the war, he was to name his newly-built house after it. Alfred and Mary brought the bricks for their new house from the ruins of one of the canal locks close by the cottage of Nelus' father, Ephraim, on the by then long-disused Wilts and Berks canal. These they hauled by hand-cart the mile or so back to their piece of land in the centre of the village, and utilised along with the stone from a ruined cottage nearby, which they had bought for twelve pounds, and demolished, and which previously had been the home of old Mark Titcombe and his forebears for centuries. Amongst the ruins of this cottage was a weather-beaten tablet which bore the date 1671, which Alfred inserted in the north wall of his new house, and carved his own plaque with the name of Ranikhet for the front wall. In all, the house cost Alfred and Mary £500 to build.

The village mason at that time was none other than Nelus' uncle (Ephraim's brother) Jesse Head, and he was employed by Alfred in the construction of the house. The following is an extract describing the building of Ranikhet, from "Alfred Williams, His Life and Work", the biography by Leonard Clark, which indicates that Jesse was of a somewhat similar character to his brother Ephraim!

On the 3rd April 1920, the walls were started. The local stonemason whom Williams had in mind appeared on the scene, being engaged to do all the expert masoning. This man was the 72 year old Jesse Head, formerly employed in the Swindon railway works. He was an able craftsman but very obstinate, and there was friction between him and Williams from the beginning of their contract. The old man praised the foundations, but insisted on being allowed to do the remainder of the work in his own way, threatening on several occasions to resign if anyone

Alfred Williams and his wife Mary

interfered. Not wishing to lose him, Williams gave him a free hand and consented to act as a labourer under his direction, but when the opportunity arose, and the mason was absent, Williams altered parts of the building to suit himself. Whether Head observed what had been done is not known; anyway he made no comment.

During the whole period, Jesse Head was paid at the full Trade Union rate of 1/2d per hour, with a bonus of 1d per hour when the work was

34

completed. Over and over again he insisted that he was a mason and only a mason, even requiring Williams to climb up on the scaffolding to empty a bucket of mortar which had been carried up before, and was actually standing by his side. As had been his intention, Williams did the whole of the labouring and serving, built up the inner courses, and with Mary's help mixed every bit of mortar by hand.

The walls were eighteen inches thick from the floor to the wall plates, except at the rear of the house where the thickness, in order to reduce the number of bricks required, was reduced to fourteen inches. But Jesse Head said he would down tools there and then unless all the walls were eighteen inches thick. There was a scene, and some hard words were said on either side, but in the end the mason gained his point. In consequence, Alfred and Mary had to make for the disused canal lock again, where they dismantled a further section of walls, and, during May, carted back a further 2000 bricks to be cleaned and graded..........

.........Hour after hour, day after day, the couple slogged on, hardly stopping for meals, in a determined and combined effort to get the outside work finished before the coming on of the Winter. Many a morning they started at daybreak, long before Jesse had arrived, worked all day and then continued into the moonlight, so that on the following day the mason should not be kept waiting for bricks and mortar.......But by the end of July the four walls were complete, and there was a house waiting impatiently for a roof. The two chimney stacks followed. Every time they got to a chimney pot, Jesse Head struck work and went on the drink. He said that at his age he could never climb a chimney stack until he had steadied his nerves by a visit to the local inn. When he returned, muttering and trembling, Williams had to tie him to the scaffold pole to ensure his safety, for he was a stout and stocky man. From this vantage point Jesse Head would hurl down curses and mortar. But by mid August the chimneys were finished and the carpenters had arrived. Soon the roof principles were in position.

Ranikhet still stands in the village today, and Alfred and Mary lie buried together in the churchyard only a few hundred yards away, both tragically dying within a matter of weeks of one another, following a lifetime of struggling against poverty. Alfred died first, from a heart attack, and Mary a month later, from cancer. After all their labours, they were only able to enjoy the house they had toiled to build for less than ten years.

As to old Mark Titcombe, whose cottage provided some of the building materials for Ranikhet, Williams may have removed the last physical vestige of him from the village by demolishing his

Ranikhet under construction and on completion

cottage, but he ensured that his memory lived on in a poem commemorating his life, which he wrote on returning home from Mark's funeral. The poem, which has never been published before, gives a wonderfully evocative description of life in nineteenth century rural England.

MARK TITCOMBE

Say, did you know Mark Titcombe, in the creeper-covered cot
Beneath yon elm-tree in the lane---a solitary spot---
With no-one near to speak to him, after the old woman died,
And Henry Love, the batchelor, who lived on the other side?
Who dwelt all alone, like a hermit, bent, withered, and grey,
With never a soul to sit with him and pass an hour away
On the long winter evenings, 'mid the tempest's hollow roar,
Chatting about old friendships, and the times that were before.
May-be you still remember the form that used to stand
In the ivy covered doorway, or clutching with his hand
The old worm-eaten wicket-gate, and follow with his eye
The farmyard teams and wagoners that often-times passed by,
Clad in a faded velvet coat, that came of an ancient stock,
Or one of his well-worn surges, or dingy holland smock,
Or a sack tied round his shoulders, since he was thin and old,
To shelter him in his poverty, and shield him from the cold.
Surely you've not forgotton him, in such a little space,
His pointed nose, and quivering eye, his weather-beaten face;
But there! 'Tis very likely, for the past two years or so
No passer-by had seen him stand as in the days ago;
For two years he'd been bed-ridden, before they took him away
Over the fields to the workhouse, on a bleak November day.

Ah well! We've seen the last of him. Mark Titcombe's life is sped;
He finished it in the workhouse; the poor old man is dead;
Here I am from his funeral; you've heard the church bell toll;
He's left this world for ever. God have mercy on his soul!
Eighteen hundred and twenty-six, I've heard the old man say,
And somewhere about Michaelmas, that was his natal day;
But he seldom troubled about the dates, for he never learnt at school
To read and write, as infants should, and tell the golden rule:
Instead his childish years were spent in necessary toil---
Tho old vocation of the fields, and turning of the soil,
Or climbing up the steepy hill that rises to the down,
Leading the gaily-ribboned team to the distant market town,
Or harvesting the golden crops, or apples ripe and red,
Or pulling up the stubborn roots, or milking in the shed.

Mark's family was very poor, and though the boys were small,
They used to rough it in the fields from spring time to the fall,
The good old mother went as well, and took her babe along,
And set it underneath the hedge, or lulled it with a song;
The maidens, too, though quite as pure, were not so dainty then,
But helped the herdsman in the stall, or the shepherd at the pen.
So Mark grew up, from day to day, and laboured cheerfully,
A robust and a handsome youth as any you would see;
A sober and a thrifty, too, contentment all his care---
He envied not the rich and great, but loved a simple fare.
And thus at length he dreamed a dream---a wondrous dream of life;
And, tutored with a warm desire, bethought him of a wife;
That was pretty Nelly Kempster, who lived in the cottage nigh,
Where elm and poplar reared their crowns in triumph to the sky;
But though they were constant lovers, and seemed to well agree,
They would never get married, whatever the reason be,
But lived in separate dwellings, a stone's-throw, door to door,
And kept the old engagement up, just as they did before.

Poor old Nelly! Perhaps you've seen her, standing at the open door
And her cottage packed with lumber from the ceiling to the floor,
With the rude, old-fashioned chimney, where a hundred curios stood,
Piled among the pots and kettles, and the stumps of rotten wood!
Do you mind the little window, with the rent and broken pane
Stuffed with linen and with paper, to keep out the wind and rain?
And the ivy-leaved geranium, standing in the earthen bowl
On the crazy wooden table, and the roof as black as coal?
Did you know the stools and dresser, and the stiff, old-fashioned chairs
Full of fusty books and papers, and the painted, curious wares
Ranged along the shelves and cupboard, black with dateless time and age,
And the gathered herbs and simples---lavender, and thyme, and sage,
Tied in little wisps and bunches, hanging from the rusty nails,
And the piled-up heaps of clothing, rotting in the useless bales?
Still I see them, plain and clearly, though 'tis twenty years and more,
And I seem to watch the firelight through the partly open door,
Or to sit beside old Nelly, as the winter wind would blow,
And listen to her witty speech, and tales of long ago.

I was one of Nelly's favourites, and often, as a boy,
I have crept into her cottage with a secret kind of joy,
To think I was beloved of her, whom others used to shun
As though she was a thing unclean, and loathe her, every one.
The dame was getting feeble then, and no longer cared

About her comeliness of dress, nor how her cottage fared,
But let the walls to ruin go, for never a friend came near,
Unless 'twas old Mark Titcombe, for more than thirty year.
And so, at last, as by degrees the unseen change comes on,
And, finally, we put off ourselves, and customs past and gone,
And, still unconscious of the change, and never looking back,
We drop our virtues one by one, and roam along the track;
So, by-and-by old Nelly came scarcely clothed with a clout,
And showed her bare and naked skin when'er she moved about.
"A witch", some said, "A sorceress". God bless you, no such thing!
Old Nelly's heart was warm and bright; she still could laugh and sing;
She still could tell the jocund tale, and chatter merrily
Of feasts and sports they kept be-times down at the Priory,
When farmer's crops were gathered in, and barns were bursting full
The Seed-Cake, and the Harvest Home, and Wassail at the Yule.

And so the years went slipping round, the seasons came and sped;
Old Nelly's kindred passed her by, her dearest ones were dead;
Only Mark Titcombe used to come to the poor, untidy cot,
And eat his victuals at the board, and share her humble lot:
The pair of them were stooping then, and bowing down with age;
Old time had touched them with his frost, and chilled them with his rage;
Each leaned upon a withered staff when'er they moved about,
Or trusted more to roof and walls, and seldom showed without.
At last old Nelly tumbled sick, and couldn't leave her bed;
But still no other friend came in to pillow up her head;
Old Mark was every nurse she had, her servant and her friend,
And waited on her to the last, and watched her to the end,.
I still can call to mind the day when good old Nelly died;
Forthwith the notice of her death was posted far and wide;
Old Mark was counted for a fool, a villain, and a knave,
As though he wittingly had sent his sweetheart to her grave.
Straightway a meeting place was named, and twelve good men and true
Sat in enquiry on the corpse, as they were wont to do;
Up stood the coroner to Mark, and told him to his face
He ought to be committed straight, and called it a disgrace;
He ought to go to prison; 'twas a proper shame;
And all the jurymen agreed Mark Titcombe was to blame.
Mark stood and trembled like a leaf, but never a word he said,
He didn't understand the law about a person dead;
He'd only done as Ellen wished, and what she often pressed---
To let no busy-bodies in, he couldn't help the rest.
But after the funeral took place, 'tis only fair to say,
In stepped old Nelly's kindred, who lived not far away;

Be sure, they owned relation then; 'tis like the human game---
Shun all your people till they're dead, then run to press your claim.
The little cot was put to sale, and levelled, wall by wall,
And that was the end of Nelly, her dwelling-place and all.

For years Mark Titcombe crept about as quiet as a ghost,
Leaning upon his friendly staff, or standing like a post;
He had no power to utter love, nor any words beside,
To tell how vacant was the world since good old Nelly died,
And so he nursed it to himself, and tottered up and down,
And choked the sorrow in his heart, and bore his grief alone.
Each morn, as punctual to time, and whether cold or hot,
The blue-grey smoke went curling up above the silent cot;
Each morn the lonely man arose, and dressed the simple fare,
Ate it in silence by himself, and tidied up with care,
Opened the shutters to the sun, that streamed so warm and bright,
And lit the rude interior up, and flooded it with light.
Four-square and spacious was the room, with the chimney large and high,
Where many a mellow flitch had hung in other days gone by;
The beams that held the ceilings up were half a tree, or more,
Rough, naked stones lay underneath and served him for a floor;
The walls were destitute and poor, save for the ware that stood
Ranged on the high, worm-eaten shelves, old-fashioned, plain, and rude;
A tiny print of Plenty hung, as if the scene to mock,
And underneath the other wall the old grandfather's clock.
But 'twas a dear and hallowed spot, although so plain and cold,
For here his good old mother sat in memory's days of old,
And friends had gathered round the hearth that in the grave had lain
It seemed to him a hundred years, and ne'er would come again.

Sometimes, while musing to himself, in the evening's ruddy bloom,
He seemed to see his mother's face shine round about the room,
And hear the old familiar voice he knew and loved so well,
And listen to the cheerful words, and tales she used to tell.
Again he led the ribboned team high up the sloping hill,
And reaped the golden harvest down, and laboured with a will;
He felt the warm and boyish blood shoot through his slender veins,
And chased his comrades in the fields, and played about the lanes;
Then suddenly he'd wake and start, like one out of a dream;
Without the night was closing fast, the dying fire would gleam;
Backward the happy vision flew, he ended with a moan;
The world was desolate to him, he was sitting there alone.

When April came with sunny skies, and fertilising showers,

40

Mark hobbled out into the fields among the birds and flowers,
Down by the shallow rivulet, that flowed for many a mile,
And waited underneath the tree, or loitered by the stile,
And, while his feeble strength held out, improved the tiny plot
That lay around the crumbling walls of his poor and humble cot.
How tenderly the old man watched each blade that used to spring---
The golden crocus in the bed, half blooming in the ring;
The snowdrops, and the daffodils, and primrose, bright of hue;
The little lenten lillies, and violet so blue;
The spring-flowers blooming by the hedge, the everlasting pea;
The sweet azelea by the wall, and the crimson peony.
True, he was sparing of his words; his was a quiet soul,
Slow to express a thing conceived, and dull upon the whole;
But, underneath his rugged cast, not difficult to find,
He wore a diamond of worth--- a rough and honest mind.

So, one by one, the seasons passed, Mark Titcombe feebler grew,
Childish and limp about the knees, and lean and sickly, too;
Shrunk were his thin and withered cheeks, his eyes were dim and red
Now less he hobbled in the field, or shuffled in the lane;
Tightly he grasped the friendly staff, his back was bent with pain;
A deadly fear had seized him, too, unkinder than the rest,
And hunted him both late and soon, like a fury in the breast,
For he saw his little hoard of gold grow smaller, day by day,
And wasting underneath the touch, and dwindling fast away.
Old Mark had always hoped and prayed he never should survive
His little careful-hoarded pile, and find himself alive
As destitute of all resource, and forced to make a claim
For something of an out-relief, and live a life of shame;
His rough old heart would fill with rage, and swell with scornful pride;
And often-times I've heard him say he'd sooner far have died.
At last, one morn, it so befell, no friend had seen him out
No smoke ascended from the roof, 'twas silent all about;
Then straight the neighbours entered in --- he'd had a sudden fall,
And lay as helpless as a child, stretched underneath the wall;
The kindly hands soon raised him up, half fainting, and half dead,
And ministered unto his needs, and tended him in bed.

Thus, for a couple of years and more, the feeble old man lay,
Alone in all his wretchedness, with every friend away;
With scarce a soul to pity him, or brighten up his eye,
Still hoping for the end to come, and praying soon to die.
Alas! Death comes not at our call, to soothe our weary cares,
But finds a younger bosom out, and strikes it unawares---

Leaves woeful misery and want to ply the endless groan,
And dashes youth and splendour down, and claims them for his own.
Meanwhile, the ancient cottage walls were crumbling at the base;
The crazy doors and windows shook, the roof was out of place;
The gusty wind came howling through, in a loud and dismal strain,
And whistled underneath the thatch with torrents of the rain.
Each time the whirling tempest blew, with a dread and fearful sound,
The bricks upon the chimney top came shuddering to the ground;
The rotten beams and rafters creaked, and groaned above his head,
Like legions of unburied ghosts--- ten thousand of the dead.

Thus, by-and-by, the climax came; Mark's little hoard was spent;
With sinking heart he heard the news, full conscious what it meant;
One only other course remained, and that he well did know---
To die neglected in his bed, or to the poor-house go;
And to have perished by himself, in such a Christian clime,
Would have been counted a disgrace, and something like a crime.
And so the rude official came, and formally inquired
If Mark was ready for the "House", and frequently desired
A prompt and ready answer, while he waited with his pen
To scrawl the full particulars down, and write it there and then;
But to everything the official said Mark Titcombe answered "No",
And as for Stratton workhouse, he simply would not go.

Again the officer appeared, prepared, beyond a doubt,
To bring the matter to a close, and force the old man out;
But still Mark Titcombe answered "No", to everything he said,
He'd rather die of dire neglect, and starve upon his bed:---
"Begone, and leave me to myself ! No benefit I crave;
Mine is the right to live or die, a freeman, not a slave;
Or, if you will, defenceless here, give me the fatal blow,
And lay me lifeless at your feet--- for better were it so
To perish in this cottage here, with that I love the most,
Than live in shame and misery among the pauper host.
This I demand, and you defy; then touch me, if you dare!
For never will I leave these walls to languish over there."
But while they were debating thus, a rap came at the door,
The workhouse team was standing by, there wasn't time for more;
Up jumped the Poor Law officers, and dragged him out of bed,
And slipped a woollen garment on, and cap upon his head,
And bore him bodily away, and hid him out of sight,
Then slammed the door upon him sharp, and drove with all their might.

So to the "House" Mark Titcombe came, and entered in the door,
Never to see his little old thatched cottage any more---
To die in exile from the spot he loved so true and well,
With sundry other human wrecks beneath the poor-house bell---
Whose sole misfortune was that gift all other mortals crave---
To live a too extended life, and seem to cheat the grave.
One day I called upon him there ---I never shall forget---
A sudden joy lit up his face, I seem to see him yet;
Big, generous tears welled in his eye, and coursed adown his cheek,
Feebly he grasped me by the hand, too pitiful to speak;
His poor old body seemed possessed of more than fever heat,
And like a skeleton he lay, stretched underneath the sheet.
There, sitting with his hand in mine, both natural and free,
I spoke about the happy days, and times that used to be,
And cheered him with an outward smile, although I must confess
There was a feeling in my heart I didn't dare express;
I seemed almost like a hypocrite, and felt a burning shame:
A glaring mischief had been done, and something was to blame.

.

At last the hour came round to leave, I could no longer stay;
But I promised him I'd come again, before I went away;
Alas! A fortnight after, he was taken in his bed,
And 'ere the nurses could arrive Mark Titcombe's life was sped.
They put him in a wooden shell, and proper notice gave,
And brought him over in the hearse to fill a pauper's grave;
We buried him beneath the wall, with a foot of water down,
And answered with the last "Amen", and left him there alone.
Now he sleeps in yonder churchyard, under the open sky,
Where the little stream runs smoothly down, or rushes swiftly by;
In the sweet and homely meadows, musical with birds and bees,
Rich with spring and summer blossoms, and the shadows of the trees.
There, high in the roof above him, from the square, old-fashioned tower,
The village bell, day after day, chimes out the passing hour,
And the green grass waves around him, like a sea above his head,
And never a jarring note disturbs the slumber of the dead;
Where comes not poverty nor pain, and care and envy cease;
For Death, the guardian Angel, rules with the white birds of Peace.

Mark Titcombe

Mark was a well-known village character whose cottage was situated on the lane into the village from Swindon. For all his long life he courted Nellie Kempster, who occupied a cottage on the opposite side of the road, but although they both rejected all other company but each other's, neither would make the commitment to marriage, and forsake their own independence, and so they both lived all their lives in their separate cottages, no doubt with a well worn path between! Nellie was descended from the marriage in 1750 between Thomas Kempster and Ann the daughter of our own Reverend John Head, the first member of Nelus' family in South Marston.

The village today is a thriving community with its own school, post office stores, church and two public houses. Like many a village, it has its fair share of modern housing and there is a large industrial estate on its outskirts plus the vast newly built motor works of Honda as its neighbour, but much of the old village heart still remains. Marston Lane, now called the Highworth Road, where Mark Titcombe and Nelly Kempster's cottages once stood, runs into the village from the busy main road to Oxford, and it is hard to imagine now that it was once the favourite camp site for gypsies, who used to sleep together here in a little tent, and live on a diet of hedgehogs. The church, as usual the oldest building, dates from Norman times, and is delightfully situated in the centre of the village, commandingly set back from the road by the triangular village green and flanked by the vicarage on the one side and Church Farm on the other. The oldest part of the church is the Norman Nave, dating from 1140, with most other subsequent periods represented within the building. Deeply etched into the stonework of the Norman doorway is the name of "Steven" which has caused much debate amongst historians over the years. One school of thought attributes this inscription to the fourteenth century, but it may well be contemporary to King Stephen's own reign between 1135 and 1154, as it is sited amongst scores of small crosses (now hardly discernible) made by pilgrims and crusaders before embarking on their travels. Contained within the tower is a fine peal of bells, the oldest dated 1420 and still ringing true after almost six hundred years.

Across the road stands the village school, a charming Victorian building, still continuing the same function for which it was built in 1873 by the Lord of the Manor, Mr Alfred Bell. The building replaced an earlier school structure which had been built around 1850 by a Mrs Lewis, daughter of the Reverend Rowden, Vicar of

Highworth, after she had "gathered a little money together" for this purpose. This appears to have been the first public school in the village, although a small private school was run in the 1830's and 1840's by a Mrs Litten and then subsequently in 1845 by a Mrs Rogers from the "Red House," now a private dwelling. Some form of basic schooling had apparently been carried out in the village in previous centuries, as the Parish Register records the death of one John Mondie, schoolmaster, in 1665. An impression can be obtained of the interior of the village school just after it was built from the description of Mr William Morris, owner of the local Swindon newspaper, in his book of 1885 entitled "South Marston and Stanton Fitzwarren":

South Marston school with the bell-tower being restored

As to the Schools, and their adaptability to meet the requirements of a village like Marston: They may be said to be all that could be desired - to be, in fact, model schools. They are brick built from a picturesque design, in which, however, a permanently solid and substantial character has not been lost sight of. They consist principally of one long large room open to the roof, and which is approached by two entrance lobbies, in which there are recesses for school stationary and other material, the lobbies themselves being entered from the boys and girls playgrounds; there is also a classroom, which also serves the purposes of an infants department. *The interior is both pleasing and cheerful in a greater degree than is commonly met with, a result which is mainly produced, first of all by the general arrangements, and then by a few artistic touches which are worth noticing. The lighting of the school is designedly good, the windows being placed respectively due East and West, which has the effect of keeping the sun out during the heat of the day, whilst admitting it in the early morning and evening. This is a matter too often overlooked, but when it is carried out as it is in these schools the comfort of the children is much increased thereby. Then, as to the second feature: In the principal room, on the two end walls, there are fresco paintings, which, by their bright colouring, serve at once to attract the attention of the visitor, and to give life and character to the scene. They are uniform in size - about five feet long by eighteen or twenty inches deep. The subjects of the paintings are illustrative of Old and New Testament history, as well as of two passages of scripture, the one painting being devoted to male characters, and the other of females, and were, we believe we are correct in saying, suggested to the late Mr Bell by the late Dean Howson. The painting on the north wall represents a race by Roman athletes, in which six men are engaged, and who are making, at various distances, towards the judge, who is seated with a trumpeter by his side, and is holding out in his right hand in front of him the laurel wreath for the victor. Beneath the figures, there is the inscription: 'Know ye not that they which run in a race, run all, but one receiveth the prize? So run that ye may obtain' - I. COR. ix.24.*

The other painting on the opposite wall which is illustrative of Jewish homelife, is divided into three panels, the centre one being occupied by a female seated on a bench, and three children at her feet; and below, the inscription, 'In her tongue is the law of kindness.' In the panel on the left there are six female figures, with a heavily-laden fruit tree, from which the women are gathering the fruit and placing it in a basket, the inscription below being, 'Give her the fruit of her hands.' On the opposite panel there are eight female figures standing, and beneath them the inscription, 'She

47

eateth not the bread of idleness.' Beneath the panels, and extending the whole length of the painting, there is another inscription: 'A woman that feareth the Lord shall be praised: her children arise up and call her blessed.' - Proverbs xxxi.

There is also on the north end wall a brass plate bearing the following inscription:

To the Glory of God,
And for the use of Christ's little ones,
These schools
Were dedicated,
June 25th 1873,
By Alfred Bell,
Who was laid to rest June 25th, 1884.
Be ye therefore followers of God as dear children.

The school was built to accommodate 109 children, with an average attendance in 1885/6 of 58. We are fortunate that the school records from 1903 have survived, the following being a selection of extracts giving an insight into the everyday life of a rural village school from the turn of this century.

From the school records:

1903

Annie Cross was Headmistress.
Mabel Perry - assistant.
Emily Beasley - candidate on probation.
Angus MacDonald - vicar.

Attendence was poor in January due to children having colds.

March 9th -13th - School closed - a teacher ill, managers afraid it was infectious.

May 8th - Examination of upper classes in reading, writing and arithmetic. Mr Vowles, attendance officer called.

May 25th - Edward Bowles left school having passed the Labour examination.

May 19th – "Examined this school in religious knowledge." signed Charles J.Parker.

June 10th - Report of diocesan inspection held on May 19th: "A beautiful little school in which the children are very bright and well behaved and the religious teaching is given with much care and success". Charles J.Parker.

October 8th - Mr Vowles attendance officer called. Applied for new stick for the school.
Number of children very small owing to the parents emigrating to other villages.

November 2nd - Attendence very small owing to dipheria breakout. Slate work resorted to owing to lack of stock.

November 9th-14th - No school due to Mistress being ill.

(Scripture lessons were given by the Reverend Angus MacDonald on Monday, Wednesday and Friday mornings, and he also assisted the Head Teacher when she was short staffed.)

<u>1905</u>

May 31st - Report of H.M.Inspector who visited school on this date:

"Mixed school" - The scholars are in very good order, and have been taught with much care. They should improve in grammar and composition, but in other aspects they have made very satisfactory progress.

"Infants class" - The infants are very well advanced. Signed Angus MacDonald, Correspondent

1906

April 6th - Doctor Powell visited the school to find the mentally deficient scholars.

May - Many children suffering from ringworm.

1909

May 21st - Inspection – "An excellent amount of work was presented. The tone of the whole school was very good, the brightness and cheerfulness of the children and the interest they took in the work being easily marked. The infants have been well taught and their repetition was very good. In all standards the work was uniformly good both verbal and written. In standard vii it was very good. I was very much pleased with the answering in the Catechism and Prayer Book. A very nice school." Signed H.Kinnick Knight Adkin.

Several cases of scabies reported.

June - Medical inspection. 15 newly admitted being examined.

August 30th - The scholars reassembled after 6 weeks vacation. The school has been thoroughly cleaned, the walls coloured and varnished, and various alterations carried out in the lavatories. New apparatus specified in the stock book has arrived.

September 16th - Attendance rather poorer this week owing to soldiers maneuvering in the district.

October 14th - Admitted Aubrey Leslie Cornelius Head. (Our Cornelius' son, aged 6)

1910

March - Children away owing to chickenpox outbreak. Revised accommodation - mixed 66, infants 31, total 97.

May - Many children away with whooping cough.

August 22nd - Admitted Edward, Herbert, and Robert Morse.

1911

February 15th - Head teacher received supply of gardening tools. First lesson given on that day.

June 21st-28th - School closed for Coronation.

Jul 10th - Head Teacher absent from school owing to accident.

South Marston school. Class of 1889

1912

May 17th - The education committee have allowed wire netting to enclose the boys gardens.

July 11th - Mr Sharpe, gardening instructor called.

1913

May 2nd-26th - School closed - epidemic of measles.

July 28th-August 1st - Attendance very poor - several children exempted with dirty heads.
Many children away with coughs.

October 13th-17th - Many scholars have left and new ones have been admitted owing to change of labourers by the farmers.

1914

January 15th - The managers have decided to dispense with scholars under five.

June 24th-25th - Dentist visited school and extracted several children's milk teeth.

September 3rd - Doctor Bambridge, the County Doctor called and expelled the families of three Traders, three Warrens, and three Merchants for uncleanliness.

September 21st - The Warrens and Merchants have returned, the Traders are gone to Highworth C.School.

October - A class for thatching and one for milking has commenced from 10.a.m. to 12 noon for thatching and from 2.30 - 4.30 for milking. There are nine boys in each class.

November 30th-December 4th - The lessons on milking and thatching concluded.

1916

October 13th - School received a "Backhurst Shield" of honour.

1917

January 15th - The county nurse called and sent Agnes Reynolds home to have her head attended to. Her mark was not cancelled as she had made two hours attendance.

Scarlet fever has broken out.

January 22nd - Attendance terrible. The farmers will not send their children owing to the fever scare.

March 15th - Edward Franklin has been admitted. [At the time of writing, Eddie, a well known and loved figure in the village has recently died.]

April 19th - Robert Morse, Frederick Spackman and Catherine Reynolds attended the Labour examination.

May 25th - Whooping cough prevails.

June 7th - Mr Wildern visited the school and noticed its dusty condition.

November 22nd - Dispatched four and one half hundredweight of acorns gathered by the children for the munition works.

December 18th - Dispatched four and one half hundredweight of chestnuts to the munition works.

1918

May 4th - School disinfected by Mr Hoddinott, sanitary inspector, owing to a case of scarlet fever.

August 12th - Admitted Vera Sansum, Alice Stone, Annie Bowles and Doris Greenaway.

1925

July 1st - Gardening Report. The Head Teacher's garden in which this small class of seven boys is taught measures about ten square rods. Although small, it provides useful instruction in growing vegetables, fruit and flowers. The practical work is well done, but, with one exception, the boys find difficulty in talking about their gardening work and observations. More importance should be attached to note making, cropping plans should be prepared by each boy before work is begun, and it would be useful if simple garden accounts on lines suggested at inspection were kept. The gardening notes which have been made were copied from the blackboard - not written as they should be in the boys own words.

October 8th - The schoolboys football league formed.

South Marston school. Class of 1928

1929

January 8th - Ten girls attended Upper Stratton School for a course of housewifery.

1931

August 17th - The system of supplying bottles of milk at 10.30 a.m. started.

December 23rd - A supply of slippers to be used for scholars coming from a distance who may arrive with very wet feet has been supplied by Mrs Iles, Manager.

1932

December 22nd - I Annie Cross resign my position as Head Teacher of South Marston C.E. School.

[Miss Cross was the schoolmistress here for over thirty years during the early part of this century, and by all accounts, was very strict, but according to the regular school inspection reports, she was also an excellent teacher. Part of the school curriculum was one half day's gardening lesson a week, which just happened to take place in her own garden at her cottage in nearby Pigeon House Lane!]

Miss Cross' gardening lesson

1936

August 17th - Gas was installed during the holiday.

1937

January 7th - The senior scholars have been transferred to the new senior school at Upper Stratton opened this morning. There are now twenty-six children on the school books.

1939

September 1st - When school assembled this morning the children were dismissed until further notice. This was in accordance with instructions received from Head Quarters owing to the Country being in a state of National Emergency.

September 13th - School re-opened this morning. During the closure forty-four children from Barking, Essex, have been billeted in the village. These children have been evacuated owing to war having been declared with Germany. The village hall is at present being used as a school for these evacuees, who, with three teachers commenced work there this morning.

1941

October 21st - Immunisation against dipheria. The doctor visited the school at 1.30 p.m. for this purpose (first treatment).

1942

September 25th - October 12th - School closed for potato picking.

1942

April 17th - Hot Dinners. The scheme for providing hot dinners was introduced today.
Seventeen children participated.
The food comes from the British Restaurant at Wootton Bassett.

1946

February 4th - School closed due to an influenza epidemic.

February 26th - Epidemic of chicken pox.

1952

January 18th - <u>School improvements</u> Lavatories were connected up to the main water supply. New lavatory basins have been fixed, and a new automatically controlled flush for the boys lavatory.

1953

June 29th - A teachers' lavatory has been provided.

1954

April 9th - Managers met in school to discuss ways and means of alleviating teaching difficulties owing to a shortage of room. A decision to erect a partition down the middle of the large room.

.

1961

January 10th - During the holiday electric light was installed in the classroom.

April 18th - The new cloakroom, staffroom and storeroom were completed during the holiday.

1973

June 25th - <u>School Centenary</u> Parents and managers were invited to the school this afternoon for the presentation of centenary rings.

The school continued all through the early years with regular visits from the nurse, dentist, optician and doctor. Also, in the very early days, the vicar took scripture lessons three days per week, every week, and played a very great part in school life. Great emphasis was put on Scripture for many years, and the children were regularly tested on this. The school dentist performed his duties in the village hall where the children had their milk teeth extracted. Lots of children were sent home at the beginning of this century due to "dirty heads" this of course being head lice. There was also a lot of epidemics of diseases that have been virtually eliminated nowadays, such as impetigo, whooping cough and measles. Mumps were also very common. There were also regular weekly visits from the school inspector, and school records were always checked. Gardening was allowed as a subject, and actively encouraged in Miss Cross's day, as most families grew their own vegetables which provided a large proportion of their staple diet. The school had a Head Mistress all the way through from 1903 to 1974 when the first Head Master, a Mr Emery, took over. Today, the school still has a Head Master, Mr Norman, and although the classroom accommodation has been extended by the provision of a new wing, the core of the school is still centred in the old Victorian building of 1873, and still proudly displays the murals described by William Morris at each end of its hall. The bell tower is being renovated and before long, the school bell will ring again for the first time since the early 1940's.

One of the rotten timbers just removed, marks the year of building, 1873, inscribed in pencil.

The aforementioned Mr Alfred Bell, who was from an old Yorkshire family, and a partner in an eminent firm of London solicitors, purchased the Manor House and most of the village in 1852, from a Mr Mountford, who was the local Swindon bank manager. This purchase was to have a dramatic effect on the appearance of the village, as it was his avowed intention to entirely renovate it and all of its amenities. His first project was to demolish the existing manor house, and build himself a new one in the Elizabethan style; after which he then proceeded to commence an extensive program of demolishing the old squatters cottages, and replacing them with modern semi-detached brick and tile houses. Every "modern" convenience was considered, even to the point of providing an arable field for division into allotments in order that the new cottage tenants should have space to grow their own vegetables to help see them through the winter months. The majority of these cottages are still standing, and have changed little in outward appearance over the last hundred years. These new houses, seventeen in number, must have seemed like palaces to the village people, with their solid brick-built construction, two reception rooms, three bedrooms plus the usual outhouse facilities and bakery shared between each pair, especially compared with their old one-storey hovels made of wattle and daub. These hovels were often originally built by agricultural workers on scraps of land along the roadside in accordance with the ancient right that, provided the walls of a dwelling were built overnight to a sufficient height, and a hearth built and side of bacon cooked before dawn, they could retain ownership which could be passed down from father to son. Construction was very crude, with the walls being built by driving stakes into the ground, and weaving twigs and branches in and around them, which were then strengthened and finished by plastering with mud mixed with small stones and straw. The rooves were made of thatch, the floor of stone or impacted earth, and the whole accommodation often consisted of no more than one living room with hearth and adjacent kitchen area, and a small half-loft accessible by ladder, to serve as a sleeping area.

On the death of Mr Bell in June 1884, his two daughters, Mary Louisa Ekins Bell and Clara Georgina Consett Bell, continued his program of village improvements in his memory. This mainly consisted of a substantial restoration of the church, which, no doubt like many rural churches of the period, was in much need of structural attention, and a large extension to the churchyard. As previously mentioned in Chapter One, this latter undertaking was achieved by the demolition of a row of seven old cottages. (Reeds Row, where Nelus' grandparents Edward and Elizabeth brought up their children). after having given the tenants notice to quit. Although this action was for the common good of the village, it must have been a devastating blow to the inhabitants of this tiny row of cottages, resulting in several families leaving the village, as evidenced by the drop of ten children attending the school at that time.

In 1918 the end of an era came with the sale of the Bell's estate. The following copy of the sale particulars gives an indication of the extent and value of this, a typical village manorial estate of the time, and illustrates that one family, as Lord of the Manor, could often own the majority of a village and its surrounding farms. Indeed, in some cases the whole village can be the property of the one person, whose influence on the inhabitants can almost be equated back to feudal times.

ILLUSTRATED PARTICULARS WITH PLANS & CONDITIONS OF SALE
of the

SOUTH MARSTON ESTATE

With the Manor House, Eight Dairy Farms, Small Holdings Accommodation Lands, Village Properties and Cottages

----

The whole extending to about 709 ACRES with a Rent Roll of about £1,797 per annum

----

And including some of the BEST DAIRY LAND in the County

To be sold by Auction in 25 Lots by

Messrs. KNIGHT, FRANK & RUTLEY
(Sir Howard G. Frank, K.C.B., and John Frederick Knight)
in conjunction with

Mr. J.A.Y.MATTHEWS, F.A.I.
at the Goddard Arms Hotel, Swindon, on Monday, November
18th, 1918
at 2.30 o'clock (unless previously sold privately)

GENERAL REMARKS
AND STIPULATIONS

The South Marston Estate, which is Freehold, is situated wholly in the Parish of South Marston in the County of Wilts, about four miles from the important Town of Swindon, with Stratton within

two miles.

The Farms are in the occupation, in most cases, of tenants of old standing, and comprise some of the

BEST DAIRY LAND IN ENGLAND

and are particularly well watered.

The growing Timber shall be paid for in addition to the purchase money. See Conditions of sale No.8.

Any dispute as to the ownership of any trees or fences on the boundaries between the various Lots to be left to the decision of the Auctioneers, which shall be final, and binding upon all parties.

The Plans and Schedules are based upon the Ordnance Survey and are for reference only.

They have been carefully prepared and are believed to be correct, but any error or mis-statement shall not annul the Sale of any Lot, nor entitle any party to compensation.

The amounts of the Tithe and Land tax, payable by the Vendor, and the apportionments of the same have been made for the information of the Purchasers, but no guarantee of accuracy is given or implied, nor shall legal apportionment be required.

In cases where two or more Lots or portions of Lots are held by one Tenant, the rent has been informally apportioned by the Auctioneers between the several Lots, and the Purchasers shall accept such apportionment as stated in the particulars and shall not require the assent of the tenant thereto, or other legal apportionment.

The description of the cultivation of the lands represent their present state, but shall not affect the rights of any tenant to alter such cultivation, and the lands are sold subject to such rights (if any).

The Lots are sold subject to all rights of way, rights of water, and drainage and existing tenancies, abatements and rights of off-going tenants, also to the orders of the County War Agricultural Committee as to ploughing up grass lands, and to the Timber Control Orders, 1918.

Every effort has been made to omit any building or fixtures belonging to the various tenants from the description of the various Lots, but the Properties are sold subject to any tenants right of removal, or of payment for, as the case may be, any such buildings or fixtures, etc., whether included in the Particulars or not. Fixtures only which are the property of the landlords will be included in the Sale.

The Tenants pay the rates in all cases, except the holders of Allotments.

All the Tenants holding under Michealmas Agreement and entitled to twelve months' notice received notice to quit prior to the 29th September last.

THE SOUTH MARSTON ESTATE

Important Sale

A large and interested company assembled at the Goddard Arms Hotel, Swindon, on Monday, when Messrs. Knight, Frank & Rutley, of London (acting in conjunction with Mr. J.A.Y. Matthews, of Swindon) submitted to public competition the South Marston Estate. This comprised the Manor House, eight dairy farms, small holdings, accommodation land and various village properties and cottages, and represented an area of about 709 acres, with a rent roll of about £1,797 per annum; and as the auctioneer (Mr Phillips) emphasised at the outset of the proceedings, it contains some of the best dairy land in the county. It may be said at once that the sale was an altogether successful one, for every lot was disposed of and the general opinion was that the prices were quite satisfactory. Details are appended:-

Lot 1. - The Manor House, with stabling, meadow, gardens, orchard and lodge; area, 6a. 2r. 18p.; rental £131. - Capt. Carlton,£2,600 (and £135 for the timber) .

Lot 2. - St. Julien's Farm, area (pasture), 23a. 2r. 8p.; rental £62. - Mr. A.T. Greenaway £1,500 (and £45 for the timber).

Lot 3. - An enclosure of pasture land fronting the main road opposite the Manor House; area 6a. 1r. 35p.; rental £19 10s. - Mr. A. T. Greenaway, £405 (and £47 for the timber).

Lot 4. - An enclosure of pasture land adjoining the Manor house, and two gardens: area, 12a. 1r. 15p.; rental £31. - Capt. Carlton, £700 (and £110 for the timber).

Lot 5. - St. Michael's Cottage and enclosure of pasture land; area, 3r. 33p.; rental £10. - Mr. J. Ashfordby Trenchard, £250.

Lot 6. - Gordon Cottage, adjoining St. Julien's Farm; rental £10 14s. - Mr. A. T. Greenaway, £155.

Lot 7. - Manor Farm, with Leaze Cottages, Fairthorne Cottages and Red House; area (pasture and arable), 123a. 0r. 30p.; rental £277 10s. - Capt. Carlton, £6,650 (and £330 for the timber).

Lot 8. - Dryden Cottages (two), adjoining the Village Hall ; rental£20. - Mr. E.Banwell, £380.

Lot 9. - House and shop (Post Office) with garden, orchard and land; area, 4a. 0r. 32p.; rental £50. - Mr. A. G. Trimm, £500 (and £15 for the timber).

Lot 10. - Church Farm, comprising house, buildings and pasture land; area, 47a. 3r. 24p.; rental £125; Mr. E.C.Garton, £3000 (and £150 for the timber).

Lot 11. - Rowborough Farm, Priors Farley Farm and Rowborough Cottages; a dairy holding with an area of 202a. 2r. 25p.; rental £392 2s. - Mr. F.G. Wildern, £7,200 (and £212 for the timber).

Lot 12. - Stone's Farm, a pasture holding of 40a. 2r. 17p.; rental £80. - Mr. H. Smith (Blunsdon), £1,600 (and £40 for the timber).

Lot 13. - South Marston Farm, a dairy holding, with farm-house and buildings; area, 131a. 0r.5p.; rental £265. - Mr. A. G. Trimm, £5,600 (and £223 for the timber).

Lot 14. - Longleaze Farm, a dairy holding of 89a. 3r. 2p.; rental £168 15s. - Mr. E.Lewis (the tenant), £3,250 (and £50 for the timber).

Lot 15. - An enclosure of accommodation pasture land, with a long frontage to the main road in South Marston village, area 9a. 3r 32p.; rental £25. - Mr. F.G. Wildern, £500 (and £20 for the timber).

Lot 16. - The Allotment Gardens; area, 7a. 0r. 5p.; rental £21 6s 8d, - Mr. A. T. Greenaway, £200 (and £25 for the timber).

Lot 17. - Meadow Cottage; area, 1r. 5p.; rental £14. - Mr. F. Pike £320.

Lot 18. - St. Mary's Cottage; rental £10.- Mr. H. E. Wildern, £300.

Lot 19. - Exton Cottages (two); rental £11 1s. - Mr. John Telling, £270.

Lot 20. - Elm Cottages (two); rental £12 7s. - Mr. E. Banwell, £220.

Lot 21. - Nos. 1 and 2, Manor Cottages; rental £10 8s. - Mr. F.G. Wildern, £180.

Lot 22. - Nos. 3 and 4, Manor Cottages; rental £13. - Mr. F. G. Wildern, £210.

Lot 23. - Nos. 5 and 6, Manor Cottages; rental £10 8s. - Mr. F. G. Wildern, £210.

Lot 24. - Nos. 3 and 4, River Cottages; rental £11 1s. - Mr. C. Beasley, £240.

Lot 25. - Nos. 1 and 2, River Cottages; rental £13. - Mr. H. Shakespear, £170.

The auctioneer also submitted:

Nightingale Farm, South Marston - a dairy holding of 55 acres, producing an annual rental of £100. This was sold to Mr. H. Smith (Blunsdon) for £2,500 (and £118 for the timber).

Simms' Ground, an enclosure of accommodation and pasture land, with an area of 5a. 0r.7p., and let at £88 per annum, was bought by Mr. A. E. Snook for £265 (and £21 for the timber).

The following gives an insight into the accommodation available in some of these houses and farms under the estate. Note the ample provision of a well and bake house to even the most humble of dwelling, and the cheese rooms in the farmhouses.

PARTICULARS

LOT 1

THE MANOR HOUSE

An excellent Modern Residence, built of stone with slated roof in
the Tudor Style, with Stabling adjoining, standing in well-matured
surroundings, with Meadow, Gardens, and Orchard and including
THE LODGE and Meadow on the opposite side of the Road, the
whole embracing an area of about

6 a. 2 r. 28p.

The Manor House, South Marston

THE HOUSE, approached by a Carriage Drive, is conveniently
planned, and contains the following accommodation:

On the GROUND FLOOR

Entrance Lobby with tiled floor; HALL, with stove; Coat
Cupboard, Lavatory, and glass doors leading to Offices.

DINING ROOM
23 Feet 3 inches into bay by 19 feet.

DRAWING ROOM
20 feet by 15 feet 6 inches, exclusive of bay.

STUDY
Store Room.

THE DOMESTIC OFFICES
are completely shut off by glass doors, and comprise large lofty
Kitchen, with range, dresser and cupboards; Tiled Scullery, with
sink, dresser and copper, and force pump from well with four-way
tap serving 500 gallon tank in roof, 200 gallon tank in scullery and
tank in garden; Butler's Pantry, with sink; Servants' Hall; Tiled
Larder, with slate shelves; Tiled Dairy, with marble shelves; Wine
Cellar; W.C.; Back Staircase.

From the Hall a handsome Staircase leads to the **FIRST FLOOR**
with

FOUR GOOD BEDROOMS
BATHROOM with hot and cold supply, W.C., and **SECOND
FLOOR** with

THREE BEDROOMS
Tank Room and Boxroom. Approached by a separate Staircase are
two other Bedrooms.

THE STABLING
surrounding a paved Yard, is built of stone with slate roofs, and
comprises Five Loose Boxes, each 12 feet square, Harness Room,
Saddle Room with cupboard, large double Coach-house with room
over. Garage with Pit. Coal House.

THE GARDENS
with front and side lawns, contain some fine ornamental timber,
including a very fine specimen of Araucaria.

THE KITCHEN GARDEN

which is in excellent order, has the following Glass Houses: -
Span-roof Green-house, 36 feet by 18 feet; Span-roof Cucumber
House, 26 feet in length, both heated by hot water pipes. Three-
light Pit.

THE PADDOCK

of about one-and-a-half acres is in front of the House, and at the
back is the ORCHARD, with timber and thatched

Store-house, and brick and slated Carpenter's Shop, Fruit Room
and Open Shed.

THE LODGE

is on the opposite side of the main road, facing the Manor House,
with Garden and Paddock behind.

The House is built of stone with slate roof, and contains Three
Rooms and Scullery, all on one floor.

The Paddock with the Lodge Garden contains an area of about 0a.
3r. 25p., and attached to this part of the Lot will be the STRIP OF
WOODLAND, extending in front as far as the eastern boundary of
the Lot, the total area being 1a. 0r. 18p.

The Manor House and Lodge are let to the representatives of the
late Mr. E.F. Fuller on lease for 14 years from Lady-Day, 1913,
determinable at the end of the seventh or tenth year by six months'
notice, but the present tenant is willing to give possession in the
event of a sale.

The Paddock is let, with other land, to Mrs. and Mr. W.J. Maisey,
on a Yearly Michaelmas Tenancy; notice to determine at
Michaelmas, 1919, has been given by the Landlords.

Apportioned Rents : - The Manor House and Lodge £128 10 0
The Paddock......... 2 10 0
Plantation - in Hand...... ---
Total....... **£131 0 0**
Valuation of the timber, £135 0s. 0d.

LOT 2

ST. JULIEN'S FARM
a Capital Small Dairy Farm, extending to about
23a. 2r. 30p.
The FARM HOUSE, built of stone and slated, contains: - On the
upper Floor: Three Bedrooms and Cheese Room. On the Ground
Floor: Sitting Room, Wash-house, Larder and Dairy. Pump and
Well.
The BUILDINGS comprise: - Timber and thatched Cow-shed of
three bays, another Cow-shed for nine cows, Chaff-house, timber
and tiled Stable for two horses, timber and corrugated Trap-house,
Two timber and corrugated Implement Sheds, stone and thatched
Piggeries.
Note:- the Engine Shed belongs to the tenant.

There is a garden attached to the house, and the lands are rich and
well watered Pasture Land.
Let (with other land) to Mr. W. Morse on a yearly Lady-day
Tenancy.
Apportioned Rent, £62 per annum.
Valuation of the Timber, £45 0s. 0d.

This lot is subject to a right of way as shown on the plan between
the points E and F to the land at the back.

LOT 3

An Enclosure of Pasture Land
being No. 158 and part 155 on Plan, and embracing an area of
about
6a. 1r. 35p.

The lot has a frontage to the main road immediately opposite the
Manor House, and will include a small part of the Plantation
facing the road where it abuts on the lot.
On the lot is an Enclosed Yard with timber-built Shed.

The lot is let (with other land) to Mrs. and Mr. J. W. Maisey, on a Yearly Michaelmas Tenancy, expiring by notice at Michaelmas, 1919.

Apportioned Rent, **£19 10s. 0d.** The Plantation is in hand.

Valuation of the Timber, **£47 0s. 0d.**

LOT 6

GORDON COTTAGE

otherwise known as Laundry Cottage, adjoining St. Julien's Farm.

A substantial old-fashioned House built of brick and partly thatched and partly stone tiled, contains Three Bedrooms, Sitting Room, Kitchen, and Scullery. Detached building of laundry with pump and well.

Let on a Yearly Tenancy to Mr. James Hayward, including the small Garden on the other side of the road now included in lot 4.

Apportioned rent for this Lot ... **£10 14s. 0d.**

LOT 7

The Capital Dairy Farm
known as
MANOR FARM

together with Leaze Cottages, Fairthorne Cottages and Red House, the area of the whole being about

123 a. 0r. 30p.

MANOR FARM HOUSE

is a substantial old-fashioned residence, built of stone with stone tiled roof, and contains Store Rooms in roof, Five Bedrooms, Dining Room, Drawing Room, Kitchen,

Scullery, Pantry, Dairy, with Cheese Room over, Pump and well, Back Kitchen and store room over.

Garden on the west.

The Buildings

comprise Range of brick and timber Cowsheds for 19 cows, with yard; another for 17 cows, with yard; Bull House, Hay House, Loose Box, Calving House. Brick and slated Barn. Cake House. Stone built Cart Horse Stable for five horses with loft over. Open Cart Shed. Range of Open Sheds with two small yards. Nag Stable with two stalls and two loose boxes. Coach-house. Detached range of brick and timber Cow Stalls for 10 cows, with store house. Timber and slated Open Shed. Range of brick and slated Piggeries. The Cowhouses are well supplied with water from two Wells. The Lands surrounding the Homestead are all good old pasture land with frontages to two main roads and access by a third road. The Arable Land is one field about 48 1/2 acres in extent, approached by the road to Stone's Farm. The cottages included in this Lot are let on separate tenancies from the Farm, but lie within limits of the Holding and close to the Farm House.

LEAZE COTTAGES

A pair of stone and thatched Cottages, each having Two Bedrooms, Living Room and Pantry. Good Gardens with Well.

FAIRTHORNE COTTAGES

A range of four, brick and tiled, one of which has been converted into a joint Wash-house with store rooms over. Each Cottage contains Four Rooms. Good Gardens. Well.

RED HOUSE

A detached House, built of brick and stone tiled, contains Attic and Two Bedrooms, Front Room, Kitchen, Wash-house. Well. Coal House at back. Garden and Orchard. A SMALL PLANTATION, at present in hand, adjoining the School House is included in this Lot. Manor Farm is let (with other land) to Mr. W. E. Jefferies on a Yearly Michaelmas Tenancy.

Leaze Cottages are let to Mr. E. Head and Mr. W. E. Jefferies at **2s. 0d.** a week each.

Fairthorne Cottages are let, No.1 to Mr.W. E. Jefferies at **2s . 0d.** per week, and Nos.2 and 3 to Mr. C. Reynolds and Mrs. A. Kirby at **1s. 9d.** a week each.

Red Cottage is let to Mr. H.O.Williams at **3s. 0d.** a week.
Apportioned Rent of Manor Farm.................**£240 0 0**
Cottage Rents.................................... **37 0 0**
Total Rents.......**£277 10 0**
Valuation of the Timber..... **£330 0s. 0d.**

LOT 8

DRYDEN COTTAGES

A pair of excellent modern stone and tiled Cottages, situate at the corner of the road and adjoining the Village Hall.
Each Cottage contains Three Bedrooms, Sitting Room, Kitchen, Scullery, Coal-house and Closet at back. Well and soft-water Tank. The right-of-way at present passing the door of No. 1, and leading to the Village Hall, will be closed and diverted and a small strip of land with shrubbery thereon with a frontage to the road, at present in hand, will be included in this Lot.
This Lot will be sold subject to the right of the Village Hall Managers, or their servants, to pass through the garden of No. 1 at reasonable times, to obtain access to the coal-house and chimney with soot door and frame therein, attached to the back of the Hall.
No.1 is let to Mr. Alfred Williams, yearly tenant, at **£10** per annum.
No.2 is let, with the Manor House, to the representatives of the late Mr. E. F. Fuller. Apportioned Rent, **£10** per annum.
Making a total of **£20 0s. 0d.** per annum.

LOT 9

THE HOUSE AND SHOP

facing Dryden Cottages, being the Local Post Office, with Garden, Orchard and Land, the whole embracing an area of about
4a. 0r. 32p.
The HOUSE, built of brick and slated, contains Four Bedrooms and Box-room.

Shop, Sitting Room, Kitchen, Back Kitchen, Scullery, Store Room, Wash House and Store. Bacon House. Well with Pump. Adjoining is Bake house with Oven. Stone and thatched Cart Shed. Timber and thatched Stable for five horses. Piggeries.

Note: - the troughs and moulding boards in the Bakehouse belong to the tenant.
There is a Garden adjoining the house and there are three enclosures of Meadow Land and Orchard.
This Lot is let to Mr. J. C. Peapell on a Yearly Michaelmas Tenancy at
£50 0s. 0d. per annum
Valuation of the Timber ......**£15 0s. 0d.**

LOT 16

THE ALLOTMENT GARDENS
situate in the main road, facing Lot 15, with a side frontage to Rowborough Farm Road, being N0.73 on Plan and containing area of about
7a. 0r. 5p.
The Land is let in Allotments to various tenants and produces an annual
rental of **£21 6s. 0d.**
Valuation of the Timber, **£25 0s. 0d.**

LOT 17

MEADOW COTTAGE
An attractive Small Holding, situated in the road leading from the Village street to Stone's Farm and facing Church Farm, with a total area of about
0a. 1r. 5p.
The HOUSE, built of brick and slated, contains One Attic, Two Bedrooms, Sitting Room, Kitchen and Wash-house. Well.
There is a good Garden surrounding the house, and on the east side is a range of timber and corrugated sheds.
Let to Mr. F. Pike on a Tenancy terminable by three months' notice at Michaelmas, at a rental of **£14 0s. 0d.** per annum.

LOT 18

St. MARY'S COTTAGE
A well designed small House built of red brick, rough cast and tiled, is situated in the meadow part of Church Farm and close to the Church, Vicarage and Schools. The House contains Three Bedrooms, Sitting Room, Kitchen, Scullery, Larder. Pump and Well. Detached Wash-house.

There is a good Garden, and the whole covers an area of about
35 Perches.
Let to Mr. E. D. Williams on a Quarterly Tenancy at an annual rental of **£10 0s. 0d.**

LOT 19

A Pair of Modern Cottages
Known as
EXTON COTTAGES
situate in the Village adjoining Lot 9.
The Cottages are well-built of red brick and tiled, and each contains Three Bedrooms,

Sitting Room, Kitchen, Scullery.
There is a Well used jointly by both tenants.
No.1 is let to Mr. W.E.Jefferies at **2s. 0d.** per week.
No.2 is let to Mr. F.C. Poole at **2s. 3d.** per week.
Total Rental, **£11 is. 0d.** per annum.

[Exstone Cottage was occupied by Nelus, his wife Annie and son Aubrey for a while in 1909, and its outward appearance today has not changed dramatically from when Annie had her photograph taken in the front garden, with Nelus peering out from the bedroom window in the picture overleaf.]

Exstone Cottage

LOT 20

ELM COTTAGES
A pair of red brick and tiled Cottages situated near the Church and
adjoining Church Farm.
Each contains Three Bedrooms, Sitting Room, Kitchen and
Scullery.
Detached Wood House. Joint Well.

No.1 is let to Mr. R. Little at **2s. 3d.** per week.
No.2 is let to Mr. S. Edmunds at **2s. 6d.** per week.
Total Rental, **£12 7s. 0d.** per annum.

LOT 21

A Pair of Excellent Modern Cottages
Known as
Nos.1 & 2, MANOR COTTAGES
Built of red brick and tiled, and containing Three Bedrooms,
Sitting Room, Kitchen and Scullery. Good Gardens. Detached
Wood House.
This Lot is sold with the right to use the Well behind Lot 22 in
common with other tenants of Manor Cottages and to use, in
common with the other tenants, of the Two Wash-houses.
Both Houses are let to Mr.F.G.Wildern at **2s. 0d.** each per week.
Total Rental, **£10 8s. 0d.** per annum.

LOT 22

A Similar Pair
Known as
Nos. 3 & 4 MANOR COTTAGES
Containing similar accommodation.
This Lot is sold subject to the right of the occupiers of Lots 21 and
23 to use the Well on this Lot in common with the tenants of this
Lot, and also with the right to the use of the Two Wash-houses.
No.3 is let to Mr. Edwin Large at **2s. 0d**. per week.
No.4 is let to the Rev. Vernon Iles at **3s. 0d.** per week.
Total Rental, **£13 0s. 0d.** per annum.

Note. - The two following Lots are situated on the main road from
Swindon to Faringdon, and are bounded on the south side by the
old Wilts and Berks Canal. The Canal is now disused and as
mentioned in the note preceding Lot 13, all rights to the ownership
of the Land and Water forming the site thereof so far as it abuts
upon the Lots will pass to the purchaser of the Lots.

LOT 24

A Pair of Excellent Modern Cottages
Known as
Nos. 3 & 4, RIVER COTTAGES
Built of red brick and tiled, each containing Three Bedrooms,
Sitting Room,
Kitchen and Scullery.
No.3 has Garden to the east and also another detached Garden on
the other side of the road opposite Nos. 1 & 2, River Cottages, and
containing Pump and Well.

Note. - The Pump and Well in the detached Garden mentioned
above is used by the tenants of all the Houses, Nos. 1, 2, 3 & 4,
River Cottages, and this Lot is sold subject to the rights of all four
tenants to use such Pump and Well.

No. 3 is let to Mr. C. Beasley at **2s. 3d.** per week.
No. 4 is let to Mr. E. Lewis at **2s. 0d.** per week.
Total Rental, **£11 1s. 0d.** per annum.

Subsequently, the Manor changed hands several times, and at one
point around 1930, was owned by Van de Weyer, grandson of the
Belgian Ambassador, whose name appears on the famous "Scrap
of Paper" which the Kaiser tore to shreds when he violated the
neutrality of Belgium in 1914. The last member of this noble
family to live in South Marston died in February 1960, and the
house slowly degenerated into flats. Sadly, it is now demolished,
and the site occupied by "Manor Close" a new housing estate.

On 31st December 1800, an Act of Parliament was passed to take
account of the population of Great Britain, and South Marston
produced a total of 252 inhabitants. By 1812, this total had grown
to 288, 130 males and 158 females, as accounted by Thomas
Godwin, the additional overseer, and Edward Rowden, who was
the vicar at that time. The same Mr Rowden had noted in the
Highworth Baptism Book four years previously in 1808, the

following: "The heat of the weather on Tuesday the twelth, Wednesday the Thirteenth and Thursday the fourteenth of July 1808 was more intense than it was ever observed to be before in England - On the thirteenth, which was the hottest day, Fahrenheit's Thermometer was generally at ninety two degrees in the shade. I was informed that in some places it rose as high as 96 degrees."

For the ten years ending 31st December 1820, the total number of baptisms, marriages and burials in the Parish was as follows:

Baptisms Males   48   Burials Males   17   Marriages 31
         Females 26   Females 32
                  74   49

Ten years later in 1830, these figures had increased to:

Baptisms Males   58   Burials Males   33   Marriages 34
         Females 51   Females 31
                  109   64

It is a matter of conjecture as to how much these figures will be multiplied by the year 2000, as, at the time of writing, further considerable housing is planned for the village, bringing a fresh influx of people to the community and no doubt changing the face of the village just as much as Mr Alfred Bell's improvements did over a hundred years ago. Such is Progress!

Chapter Three

ARMY LIFE IN INDIA

Nelus would have walked every day the mile or so to the village school, housed in the then nearly new premises opposite the church in the centre of the village. His schooling would have covered the basic three "R's" plus a pot pourri of general knowledge imparted by the schoolmistress, and only have lasted to the age of twelve or thirteen. Considerable tuition time would doubtless have been lost when more pressing duties arose requiring his attendance, particularly when needed to assist his father in running errands or in his workshop, or at harvest-time when the whole village would join in the communal effort to "get the harvest home". Considering his short period of schooling, great credit must be given to his teacher's skills for the eloquence of his writing in his diary and letters, and his worldly knowledge in such subjects as Shakespeare and the classics. This is further evidenced by the numerous published works of Alfred Williams, previously mentioned, who also gained his basic schooling from this tiny establishment. It is refreshing to note that the village school is still there educating the children of the area, and still housed in and around the original buildings in which Nelus laboured at his slate. The curriculum may be far more comprehensive nowadays, but the little playground still echoes to the laughter and games of the local children as it has done for over a hundred years.

On leaving school, Nelus followed in the footsteps of his half-brother William, and forsaking the usual village occupation of farm labourer, opted for the temptation of the higher wages on offer in The Great Western Railway Works in nearby Swindon. By this time his father's business was showing strain, with the demand for his shoes being hit dramatically by the increased availability of mass produced items which, although of inferior quality, were of a more modern style and at lower prices than Ephraim could match. To follow on in his father's craft would, therefore, have not been a

78

viable option for him. The job in the "GWR" would have involved a healthy walk of ten miles or more a day, on top of a long, gruelling shift in conditions that would appear no less than appalling to our cosseted eyes today; but at least it was steady employment, "a job for life" with regular wages, more than his father, poor old Ephraim, could ever have dreamt of.

We do not know if it was the working conditions or Nelus's spirit of adventure, but in 1891, at the age of nineteen, he left the railway works behind him and embarked on a career in the Army, signing on for a short service engagement with the local Oxfordshire Light Infantry, the "Ox and Bucks," on the twenty second of September. Although both his brothers had been christened in the village church shortly after birth, Fred on 1st March 1868, and Arthur on 5th September 1869, for some reason Nelus escaped this ceremony until the age of nineteen, when his entry was duly made in the Parish Records for baptism on the 5th December 1891. It is not known why he should have missed out on this major family event in his infancy. Perhaps Ephraim and Ann had temporary fallen out with the vicar, (Alfred Williams' description of Ephraim's character would make this quite possible). Or maybe they felt that they could not afford another "family reception". Or perhaps, after four previous children and such events between them, they considered that it was "old hat," and decided to give the whole thing a miss! Whatever the reason, it seems that Nelus was left to make his own arrangements to be accepted within the body of the church, no doubt precipitated by the thoughts of the possible dangers ahead with overseas postings once he had signed up!

On enlistment, he was posted to his Regiment Depot at Oxford for basic training, and then on the first of January 1892, he joined the First Battalion (43rd) at Gosport, Hampshire. Here, he continued his training, and on the sixteenth of April that year passed the 3rd Class Certificate of Education, comprising of basic writing and arithmetic. On the fourth of February, 1893, a new adventure was to begin when he received his first overseas posting with orders to join the Second Battalion (52nd) at Bareilly in the North of India.

H.M.Ship Serapis.The ship Nelus went to India on.

Nelus in uniform

Bareilly was a long established British Army garrison, where the various regiments did tours of duty to quell the frequent minor Indian rebel uprisings that were still commonplace in this area. In between the bouts of fighting, the Army arranged a comprehensive program of diversions to occupy the men's time. This consisted of a wide range of sporting activities, including a football league, polo tournaments, horse racing of various forms, and shooting competitions, the latter, of course, providing diversion with practical training. A major event in the calendar was the sports day held each year on the eighteenth of June, to commemorate the battle of Waterloo. Here the events included such team and individual sports as tug-of-war, races over various distances, long and high jump, swimming, shooting and even an egg and spoon race. Some of the officers had their families with them, and so games for the children were also included. Some of the events were open to all, whilst others, such as shooting, were strictly segregated into officers and other ranks, for example, the "Officer's Side Gun" tournament. The results of all events were carefully tabulated in the annual regimental chronicle each year. In addition to the annual sports day, various other regular events were held, including The Bareilly Open Gymkhana and the Bareilly Sky Races (horse racing) held in January, the Calcutta Military Tournament held in February, and cricket, football and polo matches which were held throughout the year. Whether Nelus took part in any of these events remains a mystery; certainly his name does not appear amongst those of the winners listed in the Regimental Chronicles. There were also sundry social occasions, particularly for the officers and their families, the highlight being the annual Regimental Dinner.

One very popular pastime of the period that the officers enjoyed, which would seem abhorrent to us now, was "Pig Sticking." An officer, Mr P. Osborne, gives us the following account of this "sport" taken from the Regimental Chronicle of that year:

PIG-STICKING AT BAREILLY, 1896

This has been a memorable season, and some account of it may be interesting to our many keen pig-stickers at home, although I am afraid that to those who do not know the people or the country, one run reads very much like another. We were able to begin early, the country being drier and the grass lighter than usual, on account of the scantiness of last year's rain. Our total bag was 128 boars, which is a record for Bareilly, the previous best being 71 last year. Our luck was due chiefly to our keen Honorary Secretary, Wheatley (R.A), who discovered some splendid new country down towards the Ganges, about 60 miles away, and here we got 51 boars, in the best of all pig-sticking country - fairly heavy grass, in which sometimes you can see the pigs' black back streaking along in front, and sometimes you cannot, when the only thing to do is to follow the line of moving grass.

Our fatal accidents to horseflesh have been only two, unluckily both happening to Wheatley; a country-bred mare of his dropped both fore feet into a very small open ditch, turned right over, and broke her neck; she had carried Crum well all last year. The other accident happened to a fine Waler of Wheatley's, which came down in a hole and broke his back; this horse walked two miles back to camp, and stood there for three days, when he fell down, and, as he was obviously dying, was shot; a post mortem showed that his back was dislocated.

At Behari, about 30 miles north of Bareilly, on the border of the Terai, famed for its stout-hearted pig, we found the best fighter I have ever seen. We put him up in some high grass on the riverbank, through which we were riding in line with the beaters. Very angry at being disturbed, he looked round for an object for his wrath, and spied me riding slowly along on the left of the line. He charged at once; I heard a warning shout, and, looking round, saw the pig at my pony's quarters; I rammed in my spurs, and had to go "best pace" for 50 yards before I had even room to jink. I have seen it stated that one of the disadvantages of the long spear, which we ride with, is that you cannot use it behind you; certainly in this case I could not use mine, but I think that with the short jobbing spear one would be as likely to job it into one's horse's hind leg as into the pig. To return to our boar: he was soon speared by one of the party, who luckily left his spear in, which was very useful, both in hampering the pig and in showing us his whereabouts in the long grass to which he now retired. We could not spear in this, but with the help of the elephants we so worried and hustled him that he broke and gave us a long run by the river bank, and then crossed into some light grass on the other side, where we got on terms with him, and then the fun began.

We speared several times, and on each occasion he charged well home, cutting two ponies, and appearing to be quite immortal. Self-satisfied, our hero took up his quarters in a tuft of thick grass, through which we rode repeatedly, generally spearing, and always getting a charge. Eventually he began to fail, when we dismounted, and finished him on *foot. He stood 32.5 inches at the shoulder, but looked bigger, owing to his long black bristles (which stood straight up), and his lower tushes measured 8.5 inches. Ali Yar Khan, our head shikari, declared him to be the best fighter he had seen in all his years of experience. He was one of those very tough-hided pigs occasionally met with, into which it is very hard to put a spear more than a few inches....*

....Although generally so shy, wild pig do occasionally become very bold with native villagers, from whom they have learned there is nothing to fear. One day, near Bihjoi, some men came and told us that a boar had taken up his quarters in a grass shelter in the middle of a field, charging at them if they tried to go in. We went out there, and, sure enough, out rushed a good boar.

One day at Behari, when pig was scarce, we had a sharp burst after a good hog deer, losing him in some long grass when we were very close on him. I have never seen one killed, but I believe they can be easily ridden down in open country, as although they have great pace, they cannot stay; but the killing of them is a tame proceeding.

It is at this place that we generally come across a panther or two in a strip of thick and high grass by the river, which they will not leave, preferring always to break back through the line before the end of the beat; we had evidence of their presence this year in a freshly-killed calf, but did not see them. Last year we tried to shoot them, but without success, which was a pity as they must kill a number of young pig........ Taken all round, this has certainly been a year to be gratefully remembered by all who had the luck to be in for the best of it.

Another event mentioned in the Regimental Chronicle during Nelus' time in Bareilli was something that would have sent today's conservationists into fits of anger; we are told that:

Captain White, while shooting between Lucknow and Barielli in January, succeeded in bagging a specimen of the white-faced, stiff-tailed duck (Erismatura leuco-sephala), which is extremely rare in India.

On a lighter note which, alas, ended in tragedy, the same chronicle of 1896 gives us the following story:

Everyone who was with the first battalion at Bangalore in 1884 will remember the two brown bear cubs brought back in a cage from Kashmir, by Major Wilson and Captain Strachan. They lived in barracks between the Companies' bungalows, and soon rivalled in popularity poor old "Jenny", H Company's spotted deer, being most friendly and entertaining little animals. Each day at noon they were let loose, when for an hour they visited the canteen, where they acquired somewhat dissolute habits, and as they grew out of the "fluffy" stage, they developed a strong tendency to attack the heels of anyone handy. Eventually it was considered advisable to place them in safer custody, and they were consequently removed to the local Zoo, at the Lal Bagh. The following extract from a recent description of these gardens will doubtless be of interest:-

The "bears" are the next to claim our attention. These are now located in a new circular bear house and enclosure, strongly barred. The bears are three in number, two Shan bears (black), and one Afgan bear (brown). This last is a very dangerous customer if opportunity offers, as I shall show. He is the survivor of a couple presented eleven years ago to the Lal Bagh by the 43rd (Oxfordshire) Light Infantry. The she-bear succumbed to an acute attack of dysentery in 1894. I believe that both these bears were harmless enough when young, and used to walk about without much restriction in the Regiment; but age or captivity, or possibly both combined, have certainly, it would seem, had a bad effect on the one now living - a piece of information which I can imagine will be heard with much regret by the gallant "Light Bobs". Only quite recently our ursine friend killed a native woman in this wise. Mr. Cameron, the superintendent, went down to Madras to spend the Christmas holidays, and during his absence some evil-disposed person or persons, as they say in the police court, stole the locks off the gates of the enclosure. A native woman, whose duty it was to sweep out the cages in the morning, never noticed that the gate was open, and, as ill-luck would have it, prior to entering sat down in the sun, with her back to the cage, to warm herself. Bruin came out, and without any warning jumped on the poor creature from behind, mauling her so terribly that, in spite of every attention, she died four days afterward. This, as you can imagine, quite spoilt the genial superintendent's holiday. He was recalled by telegram and a government enquiry was held, but nothing up to date has ever been elicited to show how and by whom the locks were stolen. The same bear very nearly killed a Brahmin woman in 1886, so that after all, I am afraid, no extenuating circumstances can be found in a plea of age and length of captivity.

Despite all this flurry of activity, Nelus managed to pass his 2nd Class Certificate of Education on the 6th March 1894, which gave him a higher proficiency in the three "R's." He continued enjoying his posting in India, passing the time with regular Army training, sports and other personal interests, until the 6th February 1897, when he and his Battalion left Bareilli in two troop-trains en route to Ferozepore, close to the border between Pakistan, Afganistan and India. The company consisted of 14 Officers, 5 Warrant-Officers and Staff-Sergeants, and 672 Rank and File, and arrived on 8th February in relief of the 2nd Battalion Seaforth Highlanders. It was not long before Nelus was to see his first serious action from this base, for on August 13th 1897 his regiment was ordered to mobilise for service against the Afridis on the North-West Frontier, and in the first instance to form part of a force operating in the Mohmand country. On September 27th, a sucessful action was fought near Kota Khel, after which the Regiment joined the Peshawar Column of the Tirah Expeditionary Force. In October they moved to Bara, and remained there engaged in lines of communication duties, working parties being fired at and suffering sniping during the nights.

Bara Fort and Camp

Luckily for Nelus, it appears that his Regiment was not in the thick of the fighting, and was more of a containing force camping out on the Bara Plain for seven weeks. Although this could not have been very comfortable, as the whole area was a barren plain covered with loose rounded stones, which made marching for both the men and their animals very tiring, at least this was preferable and safer than being in the line of fire. The terrain was so bad that the Regiment spent virtually the whole of this period engaged in

85

road-making, as well as route-marching, and practising loading transport animals. The transport caused the most problems, as many of the animals were very poor, consisting of small donkeys, and weakly ponies and mules. Many of the drivers were incompetent and had come from every line of life but that of a mule driver. Conditions were harsh, with food in short supply and the countryside inhospitable, and Nelus must have begun to wonder what he had let himself in for by enlisting in the Army; the life had been good up to then, with the adventure of a foreign country and a relatively easy work schedule, but now the real military work had begun. The long stay at Bara did some good at least, giving the weakly animals time to pick up a bit or be drafted out, and the curiously assorted drivers to shake down into their new place and duties. Quite a few casualties were suffered from Enteric Fever, which claimed some lives, and was caused by lice.

Nelus' regiment road-making in the Bara Valley

On December 7th Nelus and his regiment finally left Bara for Swaikot and then on to Jamrud Fort, entering the Kaiber Pass six days later. The following is a first-hand description of the appearance of these tired and weary soldiers:

The next day saw the closing scene of the march down the Bara Valley: the arrival of the 2nd Division at Swaikot. It was a sight calculated to impress itself deeply upon the minds of all who saw it. First came a small party of the Gordon Highlanders; a few Sappers and some mountain batteries; then the sick and wounded, most of them carried by their comrades; the Dhooli bearers having mostly bolted or been cut up, all the rest of the troops (except those forming the actual rear guard) being scattered along the long line of baggage animals. For hours the river bed along which they marched after passing Barkai was choked with animals, most of them completely worked out, while all day the sound of the firing of the rear-guard, which was being closely pressed, could be heard, and, towards the end, the smoke of the guns and bursting shells were distinctly visible from camp.

For five days all the men and animals had been suffering the greatest hardships, severe marching, cold, wet, want of food, which there was little opportunity to cook, and all the time almost continuously under fire. The result, of course, was that by the time the Division reached Swaikot they were all pretty well played out from fatigue. Some of the Companies gave tea to the men of the rear-guard as they marched in about 4.00 p.m., and very glad they were to get it. All day, the Regimental Coffee Shop was besieged by a crowd of hungry men, and the Coffee Shop contractor, at any rate, made a good thing out of the march down the Bara Valley. Seeing these war-worn warriors, and hearing their tales of danger and hard ship, could but make the fresh unused troops at Swaikot feel very small. The 2nd Division camped close below the Peshawur Column, and the next few days enjoyed a well-earned rest, feeling that they had successfully carried through one of the most difficult and harassing marches ever performed.

Amazingly, somehow during this period, Nelus managed to buy a book, entitled "America's Wonderlands - A Pictorial History", in which he wrote the following inscription:

Number 3709 Pte C Head
2nd Bat Oxf Lt Infty
Ferozepore N W P
The Punjab
India

"Dated November 1897"

(cost 15 rupees)

This book was one of the items found in his chest, and we can imagine Nelus looking at the illustrations and dreaming that he was elsewhere! Even the sweat and toil of the Great Western

Railway works in Swindon would have seemed a very soft option compared with what he had just been through. We can almost imagine him wondering to himself why he had left his safe village life at home to enlist into these discomforts, and cursing his spirit of adventure!

Indian women servants at Nelus' garrison

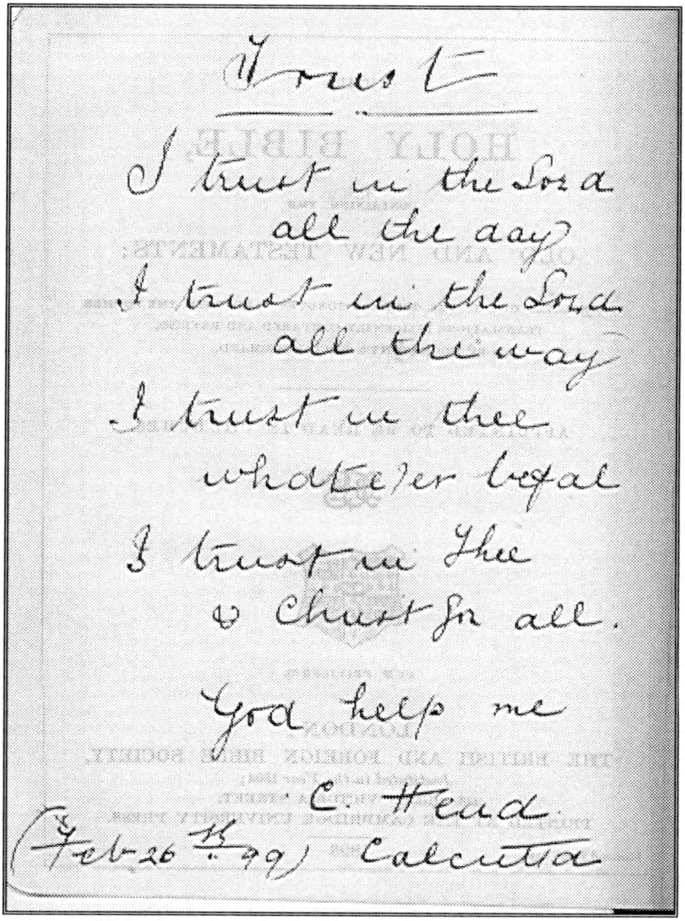

Trust

I trust in the Lord
all the day
I trust in the Lord
all the way
I trust in thee
whate'er befal
I trust in Thee
& trust for all.

God help me

C. Head
(Feb 26th 99) Calcutta

Nelus' jottings in the front of his Bible. Could
all the fighting be starting to get to him?

Nelus and his Regiment then spent the next few weeks clearing the
area recently deserted by the enemy, and destroying the fortified
villages which they had vacated. Some casualties were suffered
when the Afridis managed to reoccupy a village and fired at them
from a range of less than half a mile, but they withdrew when
further reinforcements arrived at the scene, having been alerted to
their plight by Bugler Crowhurst who had ridden for three miles
under fire back to camp. Following this, the Regiment proceeded

89

to Lundi Kotal where their headquarters was situated, and there Nelus settled into the dreary life of garrison duty, only occasionally being disturbed by the visits of rifle thieves. He could, however, reflect that the recent action had been a job well done, as is reported by one of his officers in his account in the Regimental Chronicle at the time:

This is all I have time to write now, though there is one thing that I have forgotten to mention. A large proportion of the men who had this bit of fighting came out with the last draft, and had not been a month in India. They were as steady and as plucky as if they had been war-worn veterans of a dozen campaigns, and personally (in spite of what the people at home appear to think about the stamp of men we get for the Army nowadays) I never wish to fight by the side of anything better than these Oxfordshire recruits.

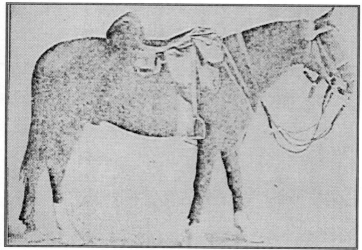

Bugler Crowhurst's pony

Nelus and friends "going native" in India

In the annual inspection of the 2nd Battalion which took place on 23rd and 24th June 1898, the breakdown of the garrison personal was as follows:

Distribution	Lt/Col	Maj	Capt	Subalt	Staff	WarrOff	Sgt	Corp	Bugler	Pvt
Present under arms	1	2	5	12	2	1	26	28	13	341
Pioneers							1			9
Musicians						1	1	1		20
Acting Buglers								1		14
Total on Parade	1	2	5	12	2	2	29	29	13	384
On duty		1		1			8	6	2	70
Sick								1		14
Absent with leave							3	2		10
In prison										4
In cells										
In guardroom										
Total strength	1	3	5	13	2	2	40	38	15	482
Wanting to complete			1					2	1	278
Supernumeraries								1		
Establishment	1	3	6	12	2	2	39	40	16	760
Detachments - Houndslow, Mounted Infantry				1			1	2	1	31

| Other Places | | | | | 3 | 3 | | 3 |
| Total | | 1 | | | 4 | 5 | 1 | 34 |

Recruits joined since last inspection, 202

Courts Martial since last inspection, 24

Nationality, English, 557, Irish, 16, Scotch 6

Average age, Sergeants 27, Privates 22 years

Average height, Sergeants 5 feet 8 1/2 inches, Privates 5 feet 6 1/8 inches

Number of men trained to Transport Duty, 37

Number of men trained as Cold Shoers, 4

Number of men trained as Mounted Infantry, 63

Number of Swimmers, 281

Number of Cyclists, 22

Number of Signallers, 8

Number of Subscribers to Library, all

Number of men attending Voluntary School, 13

Number of men married with leave, 41

Number of men wearing Good Contact Badges, -one badge, 133, two badges, 49, three badges, 7, four badges, 3, five badges, 1

Certificates of Education, 1st Class, 11, 2nd Class, 137, 3rd Class, 44

Amount of Deposits in the Savings Bank, £318.18s.5d

Number of Regimental Children, 51

Six months later, on 1st December 1898, Nelus was transferred to the Army Reserve back in Ferozepore, where he remained for almost a year. During this time, he managed to take some leave to explore the area, collecting such souvenirs as hand-worked Indian carpets, and gifts for his family. He returned to England in time to be discharged on 3rd December 1899, only to find that he was recalled to join the Colours the very next day. According to his service record, he was "posted to Details", which meant he was called up to fight in the Boer War. After having completed eight years of overseas service, he only had a short break of seven days at home before having to report to the Regimental Barracks at Cowley, Oxford on the 11th December. Although he does not admit to it in his writings, both he and his family must have been very disappointed that they only had one short week together, after having been apart for so long. Nelus' last tour of duty had involved some active service, but this was full-scale war that he was now embarking on, and there was bound to have been some upset and apprehension all round.

Colleague from different regiment in India

We will let Nelus tell you in his own words of his experiences in the Boer War through the complete transcript of his diary in the following chapter.

Chapter Four

NELUS' DIARY

A SHORT
DIARY OF

MY EXPERIENCE IN
SOUTH AFRICA

BY
CORNELIUS HEAD
SOUTH MARSTON

1901

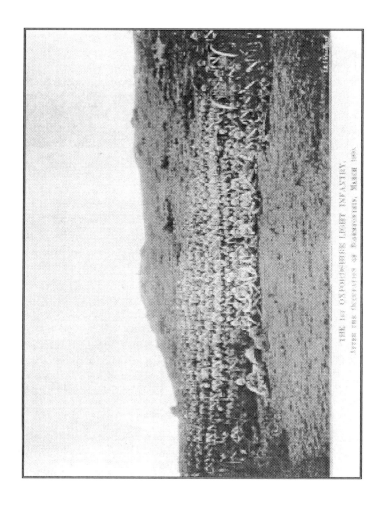

THE OXFORDSHIRE LIGHT INFANTRY.

WITH THE INFANTRY ON BANBOROUGH MOOR, 1893.

PREFACE

It is not without some slight feelings of apprehension that I submit the following imperfect work to the reader for his perusal. It will be objected to by some, I expect, that I have confined my remarks to so small a compass, thereby excluding that larger interest which several of my friends anticipated of me. But this omission was necessary. I admit that the sketch is incomplete - that it lacks the fullness of thought and comprehensiveness essential to a finished or even a moderate, composition. But this is not the result of a limited sphere of action; rather it is the result of my own inability to present things as they actually appear. An author, to be successful in the rendering of his images, must be possessed of a kind of magic. Then he must be somewhat of an artist; he must practice the same lucid colouring, only with a greater variety of surprising forms and likenesses, as the artist employs in his picture. Indeed, I do conceive the pen to surpass the brush in the vivid representation of objects and events, for art operates by easy stages; words by sharp impulse. The contemplation of art is a mere passive representation; the study of a fine piece of poetry, or prose, hurries the mind into a violent and splendid emotion, and raises it to the highest pitch of sublimity. Art is imitative, and therefore imperfect; language is Nature itself. In art the light is dim, and chiefly disappointing; but the fire of poetry burns and illumines till the very end. It is as if we are caught by a sudden impulse, and hurried on to such an exquisite state of sensibility that the mind is unable to support it, and finally languishes under the oppression of a glorious enchantment.

It is not beside my present purpose to enquire further into the dissimilitudes of what we may reasonably call physical and mental art, for, whatever nice distinctions we may chose to make, or how diligently soever we seek after some time-honoured expedient, which may seem to warrant the adoption of any particular idea into our work, it cannot be an apology for the thing itself, which, as Mr. Locke has aptly said, "must stand or fall by its own worth, or the reader's fancy." The critical reader will, I expect, discover many inaccuracies when he comes to peruse this, my first essay, to a finish; but I would warn him not to be over zealous in his search for defects, lest he pile up such a heap of them as shall dissuade me from any future and like enterprise. In the general order of my diary I have been guided by Pepys and Evelyn, whose delicious records will go down to posterity side by side with the greatest geniuses of their age. The use of the tenses has been purely arbitrary. Whenever I thought it expedient to change one for the other I did so, my object being not so much a mathematical exactness of phrase as a clear and intelligible account of things and people as I actually saw them.

C.H

South Marston
March 1901.

MY EXPERIENCE IN SOUTH AFRICA

The War in South Africa had been in progress nearly two months when I received orders from the Government to rejoin my regiment, and prepare for immediate service in the field. Of course, everybody is acquainted with the circumstances which preceded the outbreak. And if they are not, I do not propose to enlighten them, as I would not consider it to be my duty; besides, it would be inconsistent with my object, which is to write a short history of my own experience, and leave all matters of polity out of the question. It may have been this, or it may have been that, and it may have been something entirely different to either for all I know, for I am no expert in these matters, but like many others, I am forced to form my opinions from material supplied by the Press or by that other agent - Conjecture. Then, there is another reason why I should not debate on these things in my diary. Who shall say he is not running from his purpose who lays down one task to pursue another, wherein he more often becomes doubly confused than adds any great lustre to his performance. Like a person striving to follow two speakers, he has some slight acquaintance with both, but understands neither.

But to my task. On the expiration of the short notice issued by the War Office, I proceeded to Oxford, the Depot for my regiment - where I found everything in a state of great activity, resulting from the call to arms, which had by this time become pretty general. This was December the eleventh. Eleven days were allowed us for preparation, eleven days of hurry and bustle, sorting and packing, and I do not know how many things besides. It is impossible to remember all we did in that time, nor must I forget the many different hopes and fears that assailed us at times, for we knew full well the gravity of the situation, and eagerly read the telegrams as they arrived bearing news of victory or disaster. Mind, I do not impute unseemly anxiety. I do not even impute an unusual seriousness. If there be anyone who has deduced any such idea from my former remarks, let me hasten to reassure him, lest he resolve us into something less than men, and only fitted into that intermediate state, half man, half boy. But war, come when it may, or where it may, whether in the deep recesses of some far-off country, or on the very borders of our own kingdom, is equally engrossing, to one as to the other. Yet if I may be so bold as to make the assertion, and, if there be any who do exceed in contemplating results, it is they whom duty compels to take the field in person, to storm a fortification, or to repel a charge made by the enemy. Still, there was other work to be done besides dreaming on possibilities. There was our clothing and equipment to see to, this to select, that to clean and renew, and I know not what besides. For, mind you, Thomas Atkins is of the State, and the State is particular, and to be particular is to be precise and smart, active and far-seeing.

At last all was ready, and we started from Cowley Barracks on the thirteenth, bound for Aldershot. All the village turned out to wish us God-speed. In fact, I do believe that some of the good villagers were almost as much interested in the proceedings as we were ourselves.

Nor was this kindly feeling apparent in Cowley alone, but it existed all along the line of march to the station at Oxford. I shall not easily forget that day, with the steady tramp, tramp, through the mud and snow, under the full impedimenta of "marching order." The dreariness of it was only relieved by the kindness of the people who lined the way, and who made us presents of pipes, tobacco, and other useful and acceptable things. I must not here forget to mention the excellent Lady Morrell, who especially deserves praise for her kindness to the troops. There was no lack of enthusiasm in Oxford. Flags were flying, men and women were cheering lustily. Bands were playing airs well suited to the occasion, and everything had the appearance of a holiday. But, mark you, here and there you might have seen a wet face, not from the melting snow that dripped ruthlessly from rinand or feather, but with tears; tears for a husband, or lover, or a son, or brother. Think of it, you who sit composedly by your fireside, surrounded by all who are near and dear to you, and read with listless ease of midnight alarms, sudden calls to duty, and long farewells. *You* do not hear the flying shot and shell, and participate in the fierce struggle, for your mind is easy, and far removed from the scene of action. But others do, if you do not; for it only suffices that a dear friend be in the lines to enable them to be indeed present and sensible of every danger. And I would ask you if this is not true, and not only my imagination. But I am wandering from the track. How the crowd pushes, and cheers, and cheers, and pushes again. Now we have reached the station. The police have all their work cut out to keep the people back. "Steady, there steady! Why *will* you keep pushing forward? Back I tell you." At last we have all entrained. "Has the crowd gone yet? Not yet! But the time is drawing near." Suddenly the whistle blows, the band strikes up the regimental 'march', cheer after cheer echoes through the station buildings, and in another moment we are off, off to fight the Boers in the wilds of South Africa for "England, home and beauty."

A regiment gets a hero's send-off

It was rather late when we arrived at Aldershot, but we were met by the band of the 43rd, our parent regiment, and soon conducted to our temporary quarters, where each man was provided with food and drink, and made snug for the night. During the week we were kept busily engaged in preparing the necessary baggage for embarkation, and completing our personal outfits, while those who wished to pay a short visit to their friends, accordingly did so, returning in time for the general muster on the 22nd instant. By this time everything was ready, and we received orders to embark at once on the S.S. "Gaika," then lying at Southampton. I will not weary the reader with a lot of tedious and uninteresting particulars of what befell us during the journey thence, but will conduct him with all possible speed on to the decks of the vessel which was to carry us to Cape Town. We were all glad to escape from the hustle and bustle of the landing stage. I have often wondered since why a large number of people should congregate for the mere sake of seeing a vessel put to sea. I suppose it is just curiosity, and nothing else. What will a person not do for curiosity's sake?

The farewell at Southampton

We had not long to wait before the signal was given to hoist the anchor, and just as it was beginning to get dark we bade farewell to the old country, and turned our thoughts to the task which lay before us. Our first meal (tea) on board went off all right, after which we were served with two blankets, and instructed to retire at eight o'clock. This we did, and I for one was not sorry, either, for the busy day had made me tired, and what is more welcome to a tired person than sleep?

<u>Saturday, Dec 23rd.</u>

Rose at six, as fresh as a lark, and fell in with the rest of the troops to assist in cleaning the decks. Breakfast at eight, consisting of bread, butter, and coffee; after which all of us indulge in some amusement or other. I amused myself watching for flying fish, or counting the different steamers and other craft which are by no means few. Dinner at noon; fresh meat, potatoes, and soup - real soup. Have a walk to the saloon, and chat about the war. English beer a shilling a bottle. Rather an expensive luxury. Tea at half past four: bread, butter, and jam. More amusements to eight, and then to bed. Temperature below deck, hot; weather, fine and calm.

<u>Sunday, 24th. Dec.</u> Everything very quiet today. Attend Divine service in the morning (Church of England), and relish a fair discourse by Col. Dalzeill. Dinner at twelve. Pass the afternoon in watching the flying fish, which are very numerous here. Tea as usual; and hammock at eight.

<u>Monday, Xmas Day.</u> Up betime this morning, and after a short constitutional, present myself at the mess, where I learn that orders have been given to provide extra food, in honour of the anniversary. Everybody in fair spirits, though now and again you may see a mopish looking individual, thinking no doubt of a wife left behind, or some other relative or friend. But what is the use of repining, after all? As old Ben Johnson has said: "Care'll kill a cat." It must not interfere with "Tommy" though. What a dinner! Roast beef, plum pudding, and plenty of vegetables. This reminds me of home, with a vengeance, and helps the eating wonderfully. Spend the afternoon in letter-writing. Tea, as usual. Plenty of cake, and bread and butter. Some selections by the bands of the "Oxfords" and "Buffs" while away a couple of hours in the evening, and an enjoyable day closed with cheers for the Queen and all the officers on board.

<u>Tuesday, 26th Dec.</u> Weather very warm. Meals as usual. Nothing of any consequence to speak about today. Spend most of the time lounging in one place or another. Am on watch tonight, from four to seven. Voluntary concert on the aft deck. Talent very appreciable; good attendance. One short exercise and then to bed.

Meal-time on board ship

<u>Wednesday, Dec 27th.</u> Phew! What's this? Real wind, after a calm of four days. In the teeth, too! Now for sickness. Every lurch of the vessel produces fresh cases, old and young alike. Still they come. Am glad to say I am all right so far. Such vomiting and retching. Ugh! Meals as usual, for those whose appetites are not quite overpowered. Calmer towards evening, and warm; now close. Another concert tonight. Plenty of fun. Porpoises and flying fish on both sides of the vessel.

<u>Thursday, 28th Dec.</u> A delightful morning. Teneriffe in full sight. Drop anchor at eight, and take in provisions and some coal. A few officers disembark for a few hours only. Amuse myself by watching the natives selling their fruits and wares round the ship. Sharp traders these. No credit given. Baskets are lowered from the vessel to the boats below containing the necessary coin for the purchase, and promptly drawn up again laden with oranges and bananas, and perhaps a few cigarettes. Dinner, as usual. Anchor weighed at four. Weather still fine, and health generally good. Chat on future prospects till eight, and then off to bed we go.

<u>Friday, Dec 29th.</u> Still fine, but showery later. Very close; almost melting. Watch a course of revolver practice by the officers in the

morning. Shooting fair, but faulty at times. Orders issued that all troops shall receive one hour's physical drill each day. Pass the afternoon in writing. Another concert in the evening. Gay dog — "Tommy". Retire.

Drill on board ship

<u>Saturday, Dec 30th.</u> Weather very rough. After breakfast, today, I stole a march on the watch, and indulged in a short tour of the vessel, which afforded me much interest and reflection. How many, thought I, ever consider to what extent human invention and artifice cooperate in the building of an ocean steamer. Not many, I am afraid. But it is a remarkable piece of work all the same. The "Gaika" is not an extra large vessel. She has seen the best of her days; but is a good rider, and can beat many craft of her kind for speed and comfort. I had not been out of bounds for long before I was challenged, and forced to return to our own quarters again, i.e. my regiment's quarters. Nothing else of consequence today. Calmer in the evening. Watch, four till seven. Chatter about home matters and thence to bed - or should I say to hammock? Very well then, to hammock.

<u>Sunday, Dec 31st.</u> Cool, and rather rough. Breakfast unpalatable

this morning; no ham and eggs here. Plenty of serviceable bread though, and what can beat good solid bread, and its next of kin - butter? Bah! It's the motion of the vessel that's upset the internal organs. Up and down. Up and down. Divine service at eleven. Tackled a better dinner, and spent the afternoon in quietness. Tea as usual. Item: One steamer plying northward. Retire.

Monday, Jan 1st. After turning over the customary new leaf - which every good citizen should do, whether he intends keeping it clean or no - I had breakfast, and then composed myself on the upper deck, and spent a couple of hours in watching for flying fish. After dinner I had a game at "House", and enjoyed myself thoroughly till tea-time. After tea, we had more selections by the band, which brought the day to a pleasant close.

Tuesday, January 2nd. Very rough. Everything as usual. Lecture on outpost duty by the Colonel. No change. Cool.

Wednesday, Jan 3rd. Strong head-wind as usual. Sharks in abundance at the stern of the ship. Lecture on "Forms of Strategy" by the Colonel. More music. Retire at eight.

Thursday, Jan 4th. Fine and calm. Am weary of ocean life; shall be glad when we get to Cape Town. Everything as usual today.

Friday, Jan 5th. Very fine morning. Passed a large vessel just after breakfast. No change in the routine. Wrote two letters in the afternoon. Hammock at the usual time.

Saturday, Jan 6th. Still fine. Cleaned all my personal tackle. Busied myself in watching the games on the deck for the greater part of the day. Health good. Nearing St. Helena. Hope to drop anchor in the morning. Flying-fish very numerous. Mild.

Sunday, Jan 7th. Morning beautiful and clear. An unusual stir on the upper deck told of our approach to St. Helena, and I was soon amongst the crowd gazing with interest at each outline of the island rendered famous as the last habitation of Napoleon. I do not know why it is, but, however I spell this word (Napoleon), it seems to read "Waterloo". If I read forward it is "Waterloo", and the same backward. Yet the letters are different. I suppose the philosophers would tell us that it arises from "relation", or "association", or something of the kind. But that would not alter matters in the least. There it is, and when I speak of Napoleon, I call to mind that other great warrior, Wellington, and his ally, Blucher. But then, who does not know of that memorable day of June, in the year 1815? Who indeed! As soon as the anchor dropped we were surrounded by small boats, as at Teneriffe, each of which held one, and sometimes two dusky natives, vending their fruit, tobacco, etc. Everything was very expensive, and as Mr.Atkins is not usually possessed of superabundant means, I abstained from purchasing anything, beyond a couple of bananas. No parade today. Watch the tender bringing aboard the provisions and drinking water. Anchor weighed at 7.30 p.m., and once more we are off toward Cape Town, and the seat of the war.

Monday, Jan 8th. Rough and dull. Feel out of sorts. Would not refuse a tonic. Read, bad, till dinner time. I wonder if Ulysses was ever sick. It would interest me to have some account of his voyages from a satiric point of view. Fancy the gods vomiting with their arms folded about their stomachs. Horrid thought. Meals as usual. Item: One lecture. Retire.

Funeral of horse on board

<u>Tuesday, Jan 9th.</u> Still rough. Almost everybody sick, horses as well; several of which died today. No change in routine; life on board is becoming monotonous. Music in the evening, and then, to use the words of our great William, "To sleep, perchance to dream."

<u>Wednesday, Jan 10th.</u> Morning rough. Afternoon rough. Rough evening. One concert, as per regulation, and then - the curtain.

<u>Thursday, Jan 11th.</u> Fine, with a strong head-wind, which caused the ship to labour somewhat heavily. Parade at the usual hour. Held a long confabulation with several on the "Buffs", one of whom would persist in calling his regiment the most efficient in the British Army. Of course I teased him a bit, and told him that could never be, as the "Oxfords" undoubtedly held the palm. But all this was of no avail, for he would not budge an inch from his conviction. I daresay he will die in the same belief. Watch, four 'til seven p.m. One short walk, and then to my hammock.

<u>Friday, Jan 12th.</u> Still rough, with plenty of sea-sickness on board. Everything as usual today. In the evening the troops gave a farewell concert on the hurricane deck, for we were fast nearing Table Bay. Some capital songs and music. One comical little fellow made us roar with laughter, at the way in which he performed. For my part, I must confess it, I had never seen his equal. Some amateur theatricals brought the affair to a close, and then everybody sang "The Queen", and dispersed.

<u>Saturday, Jan 13th.</u> Very calm. After breakfast all the kit bags were hauled up from below, to be inspected ready for disembarkation. This occupied a great part of the day. Troops' health good. Passed a quiet evening and retired about eight.

<u>Sunday, Jan 14th.</u> Up early this morning. Found vessel at anchor before Cape Town, waiting to approach the jetty. Everybody was in excellent spirits, and full of enthusiasm. At 7.30 the anchor was hoisted, and a tug soon brought up alongside. There was quite a crowd of steamers and sailing vessels in the bay, and farther out I could see two men-of-war keeping watch over the harbour. At 8.30 a.m. we disembarked, and equipment was served out. We

Nearing Cape Town

were too confused to secure our own at first, so we had to be content with what we could lay our hands on. Arms and kit were now piled on the ground, and rations were issued, consisting of biscuits and "bully" (corned) beef, which did not prove very attractive to the palate after the wholesome food we had had on board the "Gaika". During the afternoon a number of guns were landed, together with a quantity of lyddite and other ammunition, ambulance wagons, military stores, etc. I here had the satisfaction of helping to unload the Queen's chocolate from the ship, if indeed there be any satisfaction in such a thing, for I never had any of it myself.

The Queen's chocolate

The "Buffs" had already left the jetty, and taken their departure for the railway station, their destination being unknown to us. Toward the close of the afternoon we also were ordered to entrain. The crowd was very large outside the station, and there was much cheering and displaying of enthusiasm, as we took our seats in the train. At 4.30 we steamed out of the station, and for the first time since leaving England I felt a sense of satisfaction at knowing that ere long we should take the field in earnest, and engage in real warfare. After four hours' jolting - for the roads are not like ours here in England - we stopped for coffee and biscuits, and then prepared for an all night's ride. Fairly comfortable, and as lively as crickets on the hearth.

Monday, Jan 15th. Arrived at Beaufort West at 6 a.m., where we were treated very kindly, the civilians especially, enquiring into our wants and needments. After breakfasting on "bully" beef, biscuits and coffee, we were treated to a little exercise, which we needed very badly, as anybody who has engaged in a long train journey may well imagine. While we were waiting, I found my companions with whom I had been on the vessel, but I had not time enough to shift my trappings into their compartment, as the order came rather suddenly to take our seats, and we were soon on the road again.

De Aar was our temporary destination. We travelled all day without any incident occurring worth speaking about, and then prepared for another night's ride, which, I can assure you, did not inspire us with any considerable feeling of pleasure. What with the ceaseless jolting and clatter, and the small facility we had for composing ourselves in such manner as to invite sleep, our prospects were anything but rosy. But, after all, I thought this was luxury, compared with what we must needs experience later on. So with this reasoning uppermost in my mind, I settled into my corner, and tried to forget everything in slumber.

Tuesday, Jan 16th. Reached De Aar at eight this morning, after a fairly comfortable night. De Aar is the general base for this district, being of ready access to all the neighbouring country. The morning was very hot. We partook of breakfast, and then, after a short exercise, started off once more, this time to Naaurpoort Junction, on the Port Elizabeth railway. That place we reached at one o'clock, and I think everybody was glad to escape the possibility of another night on the railway, After moving all our baggage from the station to the camping ground, a mile distant, we pitched our tents and indulged in a good square meal. One company was told off for outpost duty, and every man felt that he was indeed a soldier, and about to enter upon a very important and perilous task. Sand storms, I found, were very numerous, and also very objectionable. I did just make a short tour of the camp, and then I "turned in", being almost worn out by the railway ride and the afternoon's exertion.

Wednesday, Jan 17th. Up at 5.30 and found the morning very fine and warm. Everything was in perfect order. It did seem to me somewhat remarkable that, while only a few miles distant, thousands of the enemy were lying in wait for us, armed to the teeth, everybody should appear so indifferent and unconcerned. It was a security born of security, and which few armies could assume, I should think, without perfect confidence in their situation and ability. The other regiments in camp with us were: the "Wilts", "Bedfords", "Welsh", and "East Kents", with sections of "Engineers" and "Medical Staff Corps"; the whole being a part of the sixth division, under Kelly-Kenny and Knox. We were not permitted to leave the camp, nor had we any particular wish to do so, being almost all content to write letters to our friends, or lounge about our tents; that is, of course, after all the other work had been attended to; fatigues etc. The first day in camp thus passed very quietly.

At Naauwpoort Junction

Thursday, Jan 18th. The weather was very hot, and we were confined to the camp for the whole of the day. There was rather more stir than yesterday, but nothing of any consequence was reported, either in our district, or from the front. Rations at intervals, with the immortalised "bully", kept us at least active. The evening was very serene and beautiful.

Friday, Jan 19th. Still fine. We received news today of Buller's heavy fighting. He seems to have an unusually heavy task before him, and the country through which he must travel is peculiarly adapted to the Boer's manner of fighting; all of which adds to the barrier which is between him and Ladysmith. I passed the greater part of the day in fatigues, and chatting about the war. We were still without definite orders; but expected every day to move farther up the country.

Saturday, Jan 20th. The weather today is much cooler, and unsettled. No changes in camp. Washed my shirt and socks, and cleaned my tackle, and that was all the work I did.

Major-General Knox

<u>Sunday, Jan 21st.</u> Finer, and warm. Attended Divine service in the morning, and then had to clean a part of my trappings again, which I did not relish much. Several of us tried to get leave in the afternoon, but without success, so we had to either lounge about the camp, or indulge in some pastime or other. Some chose one thing, and some chose the other. I am afraid I did both.

<u>Monday, Jan 22nd.</u> Still no change. The troops now begin to show signs of disappointment at the long delay; and here I must confess that I, myself, was getting tired of it. It was as bad as if we were besieged by the enemy, only we were not molested by flying shells and bullets. Wrote one letter. Rations as usual.

<u>Tuesday, Jan 23rd.</u> Weather fine, as usual. Nothing of importance took place during the day. In the evening we received orders to prepare for immediate removal. Accordingly, three days rations were issued, and everything was soon in readiness for our departure. It was now late at night.

<u>Wednesday, Jan 24th.</u> At 3.30 we were aroused from our slumbers, and, in a short time, the right half of the Battalion to

Lieutenant-General Kelly-Kenny

which I belonged had entrained for Thebus, leaving the left half to follow later on. The "East Kents" also accompanied us, and two companies of Engineers; and our object was to repair the railway bridge which the enemy had destroyed some days previously. On arriving within a mile or so of the bridge we left the train, and formed a skirmishing party, lest any of the enemy should be lying in wait for us. We arrived at the camping ground without the slightest interruption, from which we concluded that that part was quite clear. The other troops followed in the afternoon with the baggage and stores, when tents were pitched and a welcome meal provided. I say "welcome" for what with the heat, and the long march, and the scarcity of water, we had become hungry, and thirsty, and tired. When we had finished our tea, my regiment was ordered on outpost duty; but not before news had been brought of the disaster to the Wilts, which grieved me not a little, for I had many friends in this regiment. Thebus is a scanty little village, lying between two large kopjes, and only possessing a few inhabitants.

At Thebus

Thursday, Jan 25th. Weather, dull and cooler. (I often wonder what we should do without the weather to talk about). A terrific storm passed over just before dinner, while we were helping the Engineers at the bridge, and which, for violence, exceeded any I had ever seen. The enemy was reported near, therefore we take more than the usual precautions, for it would not take an extra large force to overcome us. The water here is very bad. Fine in the evening, and warmer again.

Friday, Jan 26th. There is no trace of the enemy today. Take my turn on outpost duty, and help the Engineers alternately. One Kaffir prisoner brought in. Weather very hot.

Saturday, Jan 27th. Receive a visit from Gen. Knox, who came to inspect the bridge, which is now almost finished. Very hot. Perhaps it was owing to this that several men became sick with enteric fever, and dysentery. Everything quiet as usual.

<u>Sunday, Jan 28th.</u> The chief, and only feature of the day - if I may say it - was Divine service. There was a good muster of troops. Such as had no books were provided with a card on which the hymns were printed, and all passed off capitally. No stirring out of camp today. Weather fine.

<u>Monday, Jan 29th.</u> Stormy. After breakfast we were all put on parade, and then we indulged in a couple of hours' skirmishing, which put new life in us. In the afternoon I washed my shirt and socks, and spread them out to dry on the ground. Water very scarce. Rations as usual. We were sleeping with fifteen in a tent.

<u>Tuesday, Jan 30th.</u> Received orders to proceed at once to the Modder river. Three days rations were issued, consisting of one pound of "bully beef," and half a pound of biscuits, and then we removed our baggage to the railway station, and started of in cattle trucks. This mode of travelling was very uncomfortable, especially as we could not lie down with any ease. However, we had to make the best of it, and prepare ourselves for an all night's ride in the open. This did not heighten our spirits; but then it could have been worse, and the morning of ---

<u>Wednesday, Jan 31st.</u> ---found us still alive, and not much the worse for the journey. We stopped at Naaurpoort for breakfast, and then went on as before, riding all day, and all the next night. We were supplied with plenty of fruit by the civilians along the line, who were very kind to us.

<u>Thursday, Feb 1st.</u> Reached De Aar at 3.00 a.m., and were soon transferred to the Kimberley Line. The night had been very cold, and we were all very stiff and cramped. We rode all day without a stop of any importance, as we had our food on "board". Passed several ostrich farms, and innumerable fruit plantations.

<u>Friday, Feb 2nd.</u> Not much change. Nothing but jolt and clatter. The country is very hilly here, and desolate; and there were plenty of signs of the enemy having been in the vicinity. I saw that several of the great bridges had been demolished, and the line had been tampered with in more places than one. The weather was clear.

Crossing the Modder River

<u>Saturday, Feb 3rd.</u> Arrived at the Modder at 8.00 a.m. Orders were promptly issued to form a camp, and we shifted our baggage and trappings in "double quick" time. Heard artillery in action for the first time, which I found to be the naval brigade playing on the trenches at Magersfontein. I afterwards found that this was practised every morning and night. Here we had for company the Guards and Highlanders, two very fine bodies of men. Magersfontein, the scene of Methuen's disaster in November, is still strongly entrenched by the enemy, who seem so inured to shellfire that they take scarcely any notice of our guns. Water very plentiful, but food scarce. In the evening the searchlight was busy conveying messages from Kimberley to the river. No sign of relief yet. The Highland brigade, under Macdonald, attacked the enemy at Koodersberg today, and succeeded in preventing the junction of two commandos with the main body. Some slight casualties were reported, but not many. Spend our time in road making, and some other light (?) occupations.

<u>Sunday, Feb 4th.</u> Fine. No stir in camp today. Divine service in the morning, conducted by the Chaplain. After parade, a heavy sand storm passed over us, and literally smothered us with dust. Passed the rest of the day in lounging about the camp. Wrote three letters.

<u>Monday, Feb 5th.</u> We are still without orders to move, though reports of distress and privation continue to reach us from Kimberley. Two large pontoon bridges have been constructed across the river; one for the railway, and the other for the general traffic; so we are only awaiting the command from General Roberts. A court martial was held this morning on two privates of our regiment, who were charged with refusing to go on sentry duty. Result, six months "Imperial", and five months "remitted", in each case. Another young fellow of our corps was drowned this morning, while bathing in the river, so now we are three less for duty. The most interesting feature of the day, to us, was a general settling of accounts, a certain "remuneration" as Shakespeare would have called it, which enriched me to the extent of fifteen shillings.

<u>Tuesday, Feb 6th.</u> Weather very hot. No change in camp. The greater part of the men busied themselves in washing their clothes and getting everything ready, in case of a rapid advance. Heat very oppressive.

<u>Wednesday, Feb 7th.</u> General fatigue today, the whole regiment being engaged on the new line to Jacobsdal. Reports keep reaching the camp to the effect that the Free Staters are tired of the war, and discontented, but they do not seem to be in any great hurry to surrender, with all Lord Robert's promises of fair treatment. I expect they are waiting to see how the Transvaalers behave, for, despite all that has been said about it, I do not believe there is much real friction between the two forces. Toward the evening, the Naval guns opened fire on Magersfontein again, but as it was some distance from the camp we could not learn with what, if any effect, and the Boers seem quite accustomed to lyddite.

<u>Thursday, Feb 8th.</u> Weather very hot. Heavy cannonading all the morning across the river, kept us busy speculating as to whether or not our services would be required, but it ceased toward dinner-time, and left us quiet for the rest of the day. There was a number of wounded men brought in, belonging to the Highland brigade, which suggested close quarters with the enemy; and I heard

afterwards that there had been quite a spirited skirmish. Everybody was in the best of spirits.

<u>Friday, Feb 9th.</u> Received a visit from Roberts and Kitchener, with their staffs. Both of them inspected the hospital, and made a tour of all the regiments on parade. Orders in the afternoon to proceed to Enslin, where Lord Methuen fought one of his engagements with the Free Staters. Proceed to outpost duty.

Lord Roberts arriving at the Modder River

<u>Saturday, 10th Feb.</u> Everybody ready to move, and anxious to get closer to the enemy. For my part, I was sick of the monotonous life we had been living at the Modder River Camp, and therefore I welcomed any prospect of a change of locality; as such changes always bring a host of little incidents with them of one kind or another. I had not long to wait, for we had orders to entrain before dinner, and the evening found us at Enslin, where we left our cramped positions in the cattle trucks and bivouaced for the night; not, however, before coffee and biscuits had been issued. This was my first bivouac, but the weather was beautiful and fine.

<u>Sunday, Feb 11th.</u> The morning found us fairly comfortable, and in excellent spirits. At 3.30 a.m. we were served with three days' rations: biscuits and "bully beef", and then we started on the march toward the Reit River. This is where the trouble began. Talk about dust, and sand! We were almost choked. It was

impossible to get water. As I had been on outpost duty the night before, and only came off in the early morning, I fared worse than usual, and one solitary half pint had to last me six hours. The order in which we moved was as follows: Cavalry and mounted infantry, scouting; infantry next, in skirmishing order; then the transport - ten mules to one wagon; with the "Oxfords" bringing up the rear. Our first general halt was at Ramdam, a small village about fifteen miles south-east of Enslin, noted for two things: e.g., its isolated position and a bad water supply. There we all stopped for the night, sharing our camp with a detachment of bluejackets, who were escorting some naval guns. When the order came, "to bed", I raked a position for myself in the sand, made a pillow of the same material, and soon dropped off to sleep, being thoroughly worn out by exertion. So much for the Sabbath.

<u>Monday, Feb 12th.</u> Weather very hot. After the heavy march of yesterday we were treated with a rest, though for what reason I do not know. However, additional rations were issued, from which I gathered that another long march was imminent. Therefore, I got all the rest I could, so as to be fresh when we again went forward.

<u>Tuesday, Feb 13th.</u> At five o'clock in the morning we advanced into the Free State, French's Cavalry leading the way, closely followed by the mounted infantry. I should think our Division numbered about 12,000 men of all ranks. We crept steadily on over the Veldt, in the best of humour, while every now and then we could hear French with his artillery clearing away farm buildings, which had screened the enemy, or pushing small bands of them back before him. The skirmish lines extended over five miles, and we seemed bound by mounted men on every side. The marching was very difficult. The artillery horses could hardly get along at times, the ground was so rough and uneven. At eleven o'clock we reached the Reit river; and were soon revelling in food and drink. Of course, bathing was permitted, and freely indulged in. We were here the best part of the day, and bivouaced at night; till the following early morning, and then we set out in the darkness as quiet as mice.

<u>Wednesday, Feb 14th.</u> We had not gone very far before we had to halt to allow the scouts to inspect a farmhouse and some kopjes

which had rather a suspicious look about them. However, all was clear of the enemy, so on we went again, only stopping occasionally to let the convoy overtake us. By sunrise our water bottles were almost empty, and we had to go without any for the greater part of the morning. I did not, however, hear many complaints. Of course, here and there you may have heard a little "obscure English"; for there are those in the army, as elsewhere, who can speak this kind of language somewhat fluently at times. This by the way. At noon we reached Wag Drai Drift on the Modder, where we halted for a short rest, and some food. As soon as the order was given to "fall out," we all rushed to the river, and drank, rolled, or swam in it, each to his liking. This did not last long, however, for we were made to realise our position by the sound of heavy rifle-fire in the direction of Jacobsdal. The "fall-in" was sounded, and the "West Ridings" were quickly dispatched to the scene of operations, only to find that the M.I. had already engaged the enemy, and driven him off towards Jacobsdal, where the 9th Brigade was waiting to receive him with due "military state." Here we were fortunate enough to capture a large number of sheep and goats which the Boers had left behind in their fight, and as we had still a little time to spare we took advantage of the opportunity, and indulged in a feast of mutton, which was the first meal of fresh meat we had had for some little time. After coffee and rations had been served out, we prepared for a night march of eighteen miles, to where General French was awaiting the arrival of his convoy. It was a tiresome journey, and if by any chance we stopped for a few minutes, I warrant we were half asleep, officers included, always excepting the outposts. To make matters worse, a heavy thunderstorm passed over at about eleven o'clock, drenching everybody to the skin. The lightening was very vivid, and the thunder was deafening. The wind soon dried our khaki when we started on the march again, but storm number two meeting us, we suffered another drenching. But even this was not entirely evil, for it refreshed us, and helped us to keep awake, which was no little comfort to us. We had now covered the greater part of our journey, and were anxiously waiting for the morning.

Thursday, Feb 15th. I think it was about three o'clock when we reached Rondevals Drift. A large number had "fallen out" during the night, through bad feet, sickness, and other causes, and were left to follow on with the convoy. Some of them, however, did not reach the camp till midday. This was the hardest experience I had met up with 'til this time, but I was assured that it was but a trifle in comparison with what we must needs pass through later on. On our arrival in camp each received some coffee and biscuits, and fires were lit to dry our clothes, which were very wet and uncomfortable. Early in the morning Cronje's force, which had retired on our arrival, attacked French's Cavalry, and a spirited artillery duel was soon in progress, which was augmented - on the Boers' side - by a searching rifle fire from a kopje on the left. At eight o'clock my Company was ordered to escort two naval guns across the river, to take part in shelling the enemy from a high mound. The ground was very rough, and strewed with large stones, which caused us great inconvenience. But if we had trouble in getting them to the mound, we had far more in getting them into actual position on the top. We met with nothing but mishaps. At last, after smashing some of the wheels, and indulging in some sugared (?) phrases, we had to carry them up bodily. They had not been in use long before the enemy's horses stampeded with their stores, which caused them to retire some distance behind the kopje. Other guns were now brought into action on the plain, and several shells were fired into the enemy's position in rapid succession. Luckily, they had no guns fit to answer our field pieces, such as they had being mere machine guns, or pom poms, as they are called. In the meantime we had joined our regiment and were posted in a hollow by the stream, where we enjoyed a good sleep for an hour or so, notwithstanding the heavy cannonade carried on by French against Cronje's rear-guard. After pushing the Boer General for some distance French turned his course toward Kimberley, which we relieved the same afternoon. Cronje now tried to force his way to the river, with the obvious intention of crossing, but our artillery, retiring a few miles to the south-east, opened such a withering fire on his advance guard that he was forced to retire. It was now late in the evening. Outposts were thrown out, and then we bivouaced on the open veldt for the night.

Cronje's guns or "pom-poms" after their
capture and removal to Cape Town

A British "pom-pom" Vickers-Maxim. First used at Paardeberg

<u>Friday, Feb 16th.</u> After many days of marching and manoeuvering, we were at last to receive our "baptism", or, in other words, the time had come for my regiment to take part in active operations. Accordingly, after breakfasting on coffee and biscuits, we marched several miles, and were then ordered to force the enemy from a small village, which they had occupied several days previously. This was accomplished after a stiff fight which lasted a greater part of the day; but I do not think, even then, that we should have succeeded so easily, if it had not been for the artillery's splendid behaviour. Their vigour and accuracy proved too much for the

Boers, and they at length retired toward Paardeburg. The "Oxfords" casualties during this engagement numbered seventy. The Boers took their killed and wounded with them when they retired, so that we could not estimate their losses; but, judging from the position of our artillery and infantry, they must have been considerable. As they retired, Roberts ordered the guns to go in pursuit, and we could hear them thundering away till darkness set in and obscured everything from view. All the infantry had been more or less active, some in one place, some in another, and the total number of casualties for the day was very heavy. After resting for a few hours in the evening, we again crossed the river, and proceeding several miles toward Paardeburg in the darkness, bivouaced till the morning.

<u>Saturday, Feb 17th.</u> The morning opened very hot and sultry. We were not kept long in suspense with regard to the nature of the day's programme. We had just time to snatch a biscuit, and gulp down a cup of coffee, when the order came to prepare for a forced march to Paardeberg; it was Roberts' intention to arrive there, if possible, in time to prevent Cronje from crossing the river. The M.I. were first, then the artillery and cavalry, and the infantry next; with the convoy bringing up the rear. The pace was not very fast owing to the nature of the ground, and great care had to be taken lest any of the enemy should have concealed themselves, and prepared an ambush. Mile after mile was covered in this fashion. Sometimes we could hear the artillery searching a kopje or a suspicious looking farm house, but for the most part all was quiet and we marched along without much interruption, with the enemy only a short distance ahead. One mishap, however, occurred to the convoy in the rear of our Division. A party of Boers, who had made a wide detour, attacked the mounted infantry who were guarding the convoy, and took the greater part of them prisoners, including Major Evelegh of the "Oxfords". Other troops were immediately dispatched in pursuit, but the enemy got safely away. Towards night we halted for about two hours for a rest, and then went on as before, though exercising greater caution. This brought us well into the night; and we then stopped for a little sleep.

Major Eveleigh

<u>Sunday, Feb 18th.</u> The morning found us but a short distance from the drift, before Paardeberg, where Cronje had already arrived, and was attempting to cross, in spite of the heavy fire which our artillery immediately poured into him. This was the sign for a general engagement. Luckily, four of the enemy's guns were captured early in the morning, which handicapped them to some extent. Still, their rifle fire was very galling, and we had to exercise the greatest care in moving from one cover to another, owing to the storm of bullets. A terrific battle was now raging. The incessant "crack", "crack" of the rifles, and the thunder of our artillery, together with the cries of the wounded, made up a scene never to be forgotten. Yet there was perfect order. I did not witness any of those sights we read of in books, where everybody is represented as delirious from excitement, or else pallid with fear. Every man seemed to understand his position admirably. If the order was to advance, we advanced; if the order was to lie low, we lay low, and no mistake about it; but whether advancing or lying low, making trenches, forwarding ammunition, or anything, in fact, the performance was carried out as correctly, and with almost as much deliberation, as if we had been operating in the "Valley" at Aldershot. But there were no dead men to gather up at

124

Aldershot, nor wounded either, but here the stretcher bearers were exceptionally busy, and many a poor fellow was struck down a corpse, who, but a minute before, had been willing to wager on his security. There was Cronje, trying with might and main to cross the river, with the Highland Brigade hot on his trail, pouring volley after volley into the midst of his transport, while a part of the Seventh Division, which had effected a crossing some distance

Boer trench at Paardeberg

behind, arrived on the scene and, taking up a position directly opposite, completed the circle; thus rendering his escape practically impossible. In the afternoon the firing became less frequent, which gave us an opportunity to secure better positions. But the Boers had by no means lost courage, and continued to fire at us from out of the little clumps of brushwood with great accuracy. About four o'clock a small party of the enemy succeeded in crossing the river, unseen by us, and fixed a "pom-pom" on a small hill overlooking our hospital. They then proceeded to fire upon the hospital, fortunately without doing any damage. Upon hearing of this, Lord Roberts at once dispatched a

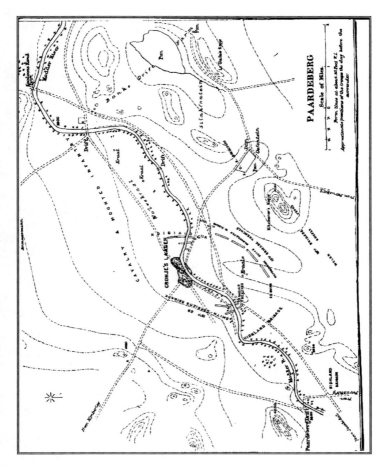

messenger to Cronje, demanding an explanation for this breach of
rules. The reply was, "that they did not violate any treaty, as they
were firing on the 'Union' and not on the Red Cross Flag." The
Union flag was thereupon removed from the hospital, and the
firing ceased. Before they could retire, however, a battery of
artillery opened on their "pom-pom", and silenced it beyond all
further question. Late in the afternoon General French arrived
after the relief of Kimberley, and immediately dispatched some
artillery higher up the river towards Driefontein. Escape was now
impossible. Hearing that a body of the enemy from Ladysmith
intended to effect a junction with Cronje, French, himself, set out

to meet them, and succeeded in dispersing them in terrible disorder, charging through them again and again. The casualties for the day were very heavy, especially of the Highland Brigade. Among the wounded officers were Macdonald – "Fighting Mac" - and Gen. Knox. At last darkness set in, and the troops on both sides busied themselves with digging trenches and burying the dead. Strict silence was enjoined by Roberts, and after a strong outpost had been thrown out we bivouaced for the night, being thoroughly worn out by the day's exertions.

The Battle of Paardeburg from the position of Nelus' division

<u>Monday, Feb 19th.</u> At daybreak all our artillery opened fire on the enemy's laager, but without getting any response. During the morning their magazine blew up with a loud report, causing enormous damage. But even this did not make them stir much, and it seemed as if they were meditating surrender. Directly after dinner a messenger appeared bearing a flag of truce. All the guns were instantly silenced, and the man was conducted to Lord Kitchener. The enemy, it seems, required an armistice of twenty four hours in which to bury their dead, but the order was promptly returned that if they did not surrender within three hours our artillery would utterly destroy them. This Cronje was not prepared to do, for though his army was enclosed within a solid wall of troops, as it were, he was yet unwilling to deliver all up into our hands, but took up the struggle with renewed activity. Late in the

afternoon we found that a small party of Boers had reoccupied the kopje overlooking our hospital, armed with two pom-poms. A battery of artillery immediately galloped into position and shelled them for an hour, but could get no response. The Glosters were then ordered to attack the hill. Advancing in open order, covered by the artillery, they opened fire with their Maxims and rifles, simultaneously, but could not make the enemy budge an inch, nor draw a single shot from them. My regiment was now told off to assist the Glosters, and I found myself in the foremost company, carefully picking my way amongst the numerous stones and ant-heaps which abound in this part of South Africa. Suddenly a murderous fire was poured upon us from the hill. We quietly took cover behind the stones and shrubs and left our Maxims to answer the enemy's pom-poms, which continued to fire very rapidly till dark, though without doing much damage. When it was quite dark we retired to the other side and tried to cut off their retreat, while the Glosters charged in the front; but we found they had already escaped and joined the laager. Water was very scarce here, and the dust was almost choking. We returned to camp at 2.00 a.m. next morning, just in time for a short nap before daylight.

Tuesday, Feb 20th. As soon as it was light the Boers commenced sniping at our outposts, causing no little annoyance, and wounding several of our men. The morning was very wet and stormy, and our clothes were all wringing wet, as we had no shelter whatever. At eleven o'clock all the troops paraded in order to demonstrate our strength, but it produced no effect beyond a spasmodic outburst of rifle fire from the laager. Upon this, our artillery made a fresh onslaught which lasted for four hours, accompanied by every available rifle and machine-gun. The Boers must have suffered terribly, but they made no sign to surrender, and answered to our cannonade with rare vigour. About dinner time a flag of truce was hoisted, and a messenger was sent to Cronje demanding the submission of his troops, but without avail, and the artillery opened with greater vigour than ever. Shortly after this the Boers hoisted a white flag, but Kitchener was in no humour for trifling and promptly ordered its destruction. Several guns were trained on it, and discharged, and when the dust was cleared away it had disappeared altogether. In the afternoon the firing wore down, and, ultimately, stopped. A demonstration was again made by the troops, but it took something more than mere demonstration to affect Cronje, who seemed to delight in disappointing our generals. When darkness set in, it found matters much the same as on the previous evening. We were still without a supply of water although the river was not far off, but the water was too filthy to drink, however, being contaminated by the dead horses from the Boer camps. At night the troops returned to camp, some two miles or so from the trenches, but as I was on outpost duty I remained where I had been all day.

Wednesday, Feb 21st. The morning was very wet, and we were all drenched through and through with the heavy rain. Food was now becoming very scarce; the most we could obtain being two biscuits a day. There was no firing of any consequence, only sniping in the morning and evening at the outposts, which, however, caused several casualties. We tried to stop this annoyance, but as the snipers were hidden in brushwood, and thick clumps of trees, we had great difficulty in locating them. Every now and then we fired volleys into the brushwood, and anywhere, in fact, where we thought the Boer were hiding. I have no doubt we killed many in this manner. After a few of these "searchers", "our friend the enemy" became quite sparing with his bullets, but when the outposts were changed for the night he was again busy, and succeeded in disabling quite a number of our men. It was still very wet, but complaining has never mended matters yet, much less has it ever changed the weather; so we wrapped ourselves up in our blankets, and lay down to sleep in the shelter of our camp.

Thursday, Feb 22nd. The weather was still stormy, and there was practically no change in the situation. A number of our men were suffering from chills and rheumatism, contracted through sleeping on the wet ground, and it seemed to me that I was about to experience the same complaint, for my limbs were so stiff and painful, and I could walk only with difficulty. Meanwhile, all the troops were resting in anticipation of the great attack. The Boers, too, were quiet, and only indulged in occasional sniping at the outposts. The day thus dragged heavily by, and by night everything was quiet, as little like a battlefield as I can well imagine, in point of quietness and order.

Friday, Feb 23rd. The morning dawned bright and clear, which was a very welcome change after the heavy rains we had experienced. The enemy was still quiet, and kept well within his laager. Sniping, which seemed to be a pet hobby of the Boers, went on as usual, but happily, for us, their marksmanship was not always of the best, else we should have fared badly at times. As it was, we managed to incur a few casualties daily, but nothing very serious. A heavy thunderstorm passed over today and flooded us out of all the low places. The lightening was terrific. The Glo'sters, who had been unlucky throughout the whole of the campaign, met with another piece of ill-fortune. A number of their men were taking refuge beneath some ammunition wagons, when a flash of lightening struck one of the wheels, and ran all round the vehicle, killing two men and burning five others very badly. Luckily the wagon was empty of ammunition, or the consequence might have been disastrous. I was close to the wagon at the time, and though I did not see the actual occurrence, I saw all the men afterwards. The remaining part of the day passed off quietly. Outposts were changed at six, and everything secured for the night.

Saturday, Feb 24th. No change in the general situation. The occasional crack of a rifle reminded us of the Boer snipers; otherwise all was quiet in the laager. The weather was very fine and warm. Lord Roberts was now completing his arrangements for a combined attack on the enemy's position, while the troops, after their rest, were refreshed and eager to fight to a finish. Food was very scarce; we were all on short rations, but water was plentiful. There was nothing worthy of note took place today, except the issue of food, which we all began to look upon as a most important business.

Sunday, Feb 25th. The morning was clear and bright, and attended with a quietness peculiarly in keeping with the Sabbath. It was an ideal scene, and I thought longingly of the simple though picturesque meadowland that lay about my home in the old country. We had Divine service in the morning, conducted by the Chaplain, and then the rest went off very quietly. There was much gossip in the evening about the coming assault; the men were in excellent spirits, and fit for anything.

<u>Monday, Feb 26th,</u> Early in the morning we were reinforced by a Naval detachment with six Hotchkiss guns, which had been sent up from Cape Town. This looked like business. Then Lord Roberts sent out a flag of truce, demanding an unconditional surrender, adding that if the enemy did not surrender the laager within twenty four hours he would advance and take it at the point of a bayonet. This, also, looked like business. But Cronje was still obdurate. Perhaps he thought that by prolonging the siege he might yet stand some chance of being assisted by one of the commandos which had been operating in the district. However this may have been, he treated Roberts' demand in the negative, and, as if to emphasise his refusal, he discharged some rifles at us, as well as he knew how. Every day our troops had been digging trenches, and advancing closer and closer to the enemy's laager; and now the order was given to be in readiness for the final attack, which was to take place early the next morning. All through the day we were very quietly getting everything ready, seeing to our ammunition, etc. Then when darkness set in we took our positions with as little noise as possible, and prepared for a wait of several hours. There could be no doubt about it; Cronje was doomed. He was enclosed within a wall of rifles and artillery. A wall of eyes encompassed him, and a wall of determination was his defence. Nine men out of every ten would have given up in despair at the knowledge of such overwhelming numbers as he had against him, but he did not. The man's nerve was remarkable. It is even said that he gloried in his position, and went about his laager in a state of unassumed hilarity. This may or may not be true, but it agrees with the elements of his nature, and with descriptions we have had of him since he has been in St. Helena. But this by the way. Never has the fine picture of Tennyson's in his famous "Charge of the Light Brigade" been suggested with greater appropriateness than here. Cannon to right of them, cannon to left of them, nothing but cannon and rifles, and the deadly Maxims all round. There was no stir in the river bed. All was quiet. It was an awful stillness; the suspense was terrible. The Canadians were nearest to the trenches, with the Highlanders only a short distance behind. These were on the Kimberley side, and were supported by two naval guns.

131

Midnight came---

<u>Tuesday, Feb 27th.</u> ---and passed, and everything was in deep silence. Nobody stirred. Then one o'clock came. Then two o'clock. Everybody was now almost breathless with excitement. But there was not much longer to wait. At half-past two the signal was given, and every cannon and rifle belched out fire and lead, shot and shell, simultaneously. The effect was indescribable. It was magnificent - it was terrible. It thrilled us with fire, it enfused us with a spirit of inhuman exultation, but before long it froze us with terror. The same reasons that lifted our spirits up, plunged them into an infinitely deeper gulf than would be thought possible by many, for we had begun to realise the true state of the situation. No man who has a grain of humanity about him can forebear a little pity, however slight, when he has the foe at his mercy, even though circumstances compel him to smother it. But duty is duty, and we kept firing away, either in volleys or indiscriminately, thus maintaining one continuous fusilade. But Cronje was not to be frightened very easily, nor did we take him by surprise, as we had hoped to do. It seems that he had anticipated our attack, and made all the preparations in his power for resisting it. He had posted his men with great judgement, and we have only to go through the heavy list of casualties in this engagement to find out how vigorously the Boers defended the laager till the very end. The brunt of the attack was borne by the Canadians; to them is due the credit of having charged into the first line of trenches, though at a great cost. All this time the fight had been raging without a moment's intermission, but when Cronje found that we had really reached his trenches, and that Lord Roberts' threat of the preceding morning had been indeed carried into effect, he very reluctantly hoisted a flag of truce, and the firing ceased. When it became known that he had indeed surrendered, we burst into one long, tremendous cheer that made the whole heavens ring. It was a welcome change - from the sound of battle to the sound of victory, and although we knew it must come, sooner or later, yet it was a victory, which pleased us all the more. The losses were very heavy on either side, and we had suffered several little mishaps through operating in the darkness, which all helped to swell the list. But there could be no blame attached to anyone. The officers had behaved admirably, and we, that is, the men, had done likewise.

At least, I hope we did, and the papers told us so afterwards. And they never err, do they? Everything was very quiet till the expiration of the time agreed upon by Roberts for the evacuation of the laager. At about six o'clock Cronje appeared with a white flag, and a brigade marched inside, and took up its position as guard, while all the arms were collected into a heap. Cronje was now met by an escort, and conducted to Lord Roberts. He is a short, stoutish man, with a shrewd countenance; somewhat stern in appearance, and having the manner of one used to hardship and the eating cares of anxiety. His clothes were threadbare and dirty, and he carried a whip in his hand which graced him more than a rifle could have done, for he looked a typical farmer, such as one would expect to meet with away in the wilds. The meeting of the two commanders was quite the feature of the morning. After a conventional handshake Lord Roberts said "You have made a gallant defence, sir!" Cronje did not reply, but looked very nervous and pallid. Roberts then asked him to partake of some refreshment, which he at first declined to do, but he consented afterwards. Very soon his wife joined him, and they both sat down in the shade of a large tree, where they conversed together without interruption. Mrs Cronje's appearance was pitiable in the extreme. Her dress, naturally plain, was now shabby and dirty; her face was thin and careworn, and she walked unsteadily and with some difficulty, like one who had been long cramped in an unnatural position. But she was not the only woman in the Boer laager, for there were many, and not only women, but children, also. Whether they had attended their husbands voluntarily, or on compulsion, I am utterly at a loss to say, though I can scarcely think that any man would force his wife and children to follow him into such a deathtrap as this. But they did not seem to have suffered much from the fire, as they were safely stowed away beneath the ground out of the reach of the shells and bullets. It must have been an awful trial for these women and children to have heard the shells bursting over their heads, killing husbands and fathers in one breath, and yet not daring to move an inch, lest they should share the same fate. I think this is one of the most remarkable features of the campaign in the Free State. Surely these women were gifted with more than the ordinary spirit of the race, that they should change their homes for such scenes of bloodshed and carnage. Incidents like these will live, when the main features of the war are

The surrender of Cronje at the Battle of Paardeberg

Cronje with Captain Watermeier (Roberts' A.D.C.) after his surrender

ignored and forgotten. The prisoners were now marched out of the laager and halted by the hospital, where each man was served with biscuits and coffee.

Some of Cronje's men after the surrender at Paardeberg

I have never seen such a medley of men together under arms at any time in my life. There were grey-headed men of sixty and seventy, others in the very prime of manhood; robust youths of twenty, and so on down to mere boys of twelve, whose proper place would have been the school house. But they had not suffered much from the siege, to judge by appearances; and if we had made a careful comparison with our men, e.g., in points of general condition - I think they would have been just the better for the comparison. As to their defence, little need be said here, but whoever possesses the most elementary knowledge of military affairs will immediately see how utterly hopeless it was for Cronje to escape, even if he had been endued with superhuman power, and assisted by artillery. But they stuck well to their post, and fought to the end. Nobody could do more. After they had finished with biscuits and coffee, they were placed under a strong escort and marched off to the Modder, and thence to Cape Town, which they reached without mishap a few days afterwards. The laager presented an awful appearance when the wounded had been removed. It was filthy beyond description. Dead horses and mules, broken wagons, articles of clothing, baby linen and feeding bottles, utensils and food, were scattered about in every direction, while the ground had been ploughed up by the lyddite and shrapnel to an enormous extent.

The scene of devastation in Cronje's lines after the battle

The trenches were simply masterpieces of construction in their way, differing from those used by our troops, as an up to date article differs from an antiquated one. I think they have since been used to some advantage by our officers.

After this summing up of Paardeburg we were treated to a rest extending over two days, and then we were ordered to prepare for a rapid advance on Bloemfontein. General French had already left, and was busy searching the country for any other further trace of the enemy.

Pile of guns taken from Cronje's men

Cronje and his wife boarding the train after the surrender

Boer prisoners boarding the train after the battle

My complaint now became worse, and I was ordered to leave the regiment and go to the hospital - much against my will - so that my diary, as far as it is connected with active service, is practically over. However, to complete the thread of my narrative, I will contrive to give a short account of my hospital experience, and the voyage back to England, even though it may prove dry and uninteresting.

CONCLUSION

As Lord Roberts was anxious to be on the move, it was desirable that all the sick and wounded should be sent off as quickly as possible, so that on the second day after the surrender the sick and wounded were placed in ambulance waggons and taken off towards Kimberley. When we reached the river, which we had previously crossed in our pursuit of Cronje, we found that only one boat was available for taking us across, which hindered us for a considerable time, but we managed it all right in the end, and then buck-wagons were waiting to convey us the rest of our journey. It was very rough travelling, and the night was bitterly cold - for we had now been riding one whole day. Of course sleep was out of the question, as the continual bump, bump, of the waggons rendered that impossible; but we were in fairly good spirits, and I did not hear many complaints. In the morning we halted for breakfast at a small camp occupied by four companies of the North Lancashire Regiment, and then pushed on again towards Kimberley.

An ambulance wagon gets stuck

It now came on to rain and we were soon drenched to the skin, which did not mend matters; but on our arrival at the hospital we were well cared for, and with a good system of food and plenty of rest, I soon regained some of my lost strength, though to cure my complaint was not such an easy matter. While I was here Lord Roberts and Kitchener, with Cecil Rhodes, paid us a visit. They visited every wounded man, and asked him how and when he received his injuries in a most considerate manner. I stayed at Kimberley 'til the sixth of March, and was then transferred to the Orange River Hospital. On the way to this place we had to pass Magersfontein, where the Highland Brigade, under Lord Methuen, came to grief. The trenches, for the most part, still intact; but an air of desolation seemed to hang over the place, and I was not sorry to leave it all behind me. We stopped for a few moments at the Modder - another place rendered famous in history - and then we soon reached the hospital. After two days of ease and comfort, I was again removed, this time to Cape Town, so that I had to bid farewell to the scene of warfare, altogether. The journey down was very uncomfortable. There were twenty-five of us in one truck, and the room was so limited that we could scarcely sit down. Lying down was out of the question. Biscuits formed our complete diet, besides what the civilians gave us when we halted at a station to take water or fuel. They were, indeed, kind to us, and gave us all kinds of fruit, tobacco, cigarettes and other dainties. We stopped at Beaufort West for breakfast on the ninth, after an all night ride, and reached Salt River at noon.

Beaufort West

Here we were shunted on to the branch line, and a few minutes brought us to our final destination. Rondesbosch Hospital is situated in a fine healthy spot some little distance from Cape Town, commanding a fine view over Table Mountain and possessed of unlimited accommodation. Of course, like all other temporary hospitals, it was only composed of tents and marquees, but then this is only a secondary matter, where the climate is so healthy and uniform.

Rondesbosch Hospital

The first day or two passed off very quietly. We were all too tired to stir much, even if we had been so inclined; so we spent our time in lying down, or lounging, if they are not one and the same thing. At least, the difference is not very general. The treatment everywhere was excellent. All that a sick soldier required he could have without stint. The residents in the neighbourhood were very kind, and kept us constantly supplied with luxuries of one sort and another, which we greatly appreciated. Then we had a real troupe of minstrels belonging to the camp, and these provided a concert every week, which kept us from getting too melancholy. Taking everything into consideration, we had a very good time of it.

Hospital nurses

Sick and wounded men were being brought in every week from the front; some suffering from enteric, some from dysentery, and others from wounds. It was a pitiable sight to see the poor fellows arrive from the train. When a patient becomes convalescent he is sent to Green Point, a fine healthy station close to the sea, and if he recovers sufficiently he is sent back to the front. It is here the Boer prisoners are kept - those, at least, who are not sent to St. Helena. They are completely surrounded by barbed wire fences, and guarded day and night by a large number of sentries having loaded rifles. At night their camp is lit up by electricity, so that there shall be no trouble in watching their movements. While I was at Rondesbosch, one young Boer was shot in attempting to escape. There was some dispute about the case, and an inquiry was held, but the young fellow who shot him, a private in the Warwick Militia, was honourably acquitted in the end, and promoted to the rank of corporal.

Nelus (middle row, far right) at Rondesbosch Hospital

Early in April I was discharged from the hospital, and attached to the Medical Staff Corps. Occasionally, I helped in the kitchen, when the work was very heavy, but I did not exert myself beyond the ordinary duties. In May we had wooden huts to live in, instead of the tents. Of course, I followed the doings of my regiment with more than ordinary interest; and was greatly pleased with the manner in which they behaved in the field. On Mafeking night we had a grand concert in honour of Baden-Powell. There was great rejoicing all through the Colony, but especially in Cape Town, where the bands paraded the streets nearly all day, followed by a large crowd bearing Kruger's effigy. A week later we had another general holiday, it being the Queen's birthday. All the troops paraded. Guns were fired at intervals from the harbour and forts, and in the evening we had plenty of enjoyment. The weather was particularly fine and genial. From May to August the days slipped by without much occurring worthy of mention, and then I helped to escort a batch of prisoners to East London by steamer, they being on their way to Ceylon. The weather was fine during the whole of the voyage, but there was no incident, and matters seemed to assume a kind of humdrum and uninteresting way of procedure. Things continued in this manner till the twentieth of October, and then I was ordered to prepare for England. You may imagine how pleased I was to receive such a piece of news. It was what I had been longing for. There were 820 of us to go, and in "double-quick" time we were placed on board the "Tages" mail boat, bound for Southampton, and the next day we put out to sea. The vessel was very clean, but the discipline was slack, and the food was truly abominable, especially when it is remembered that the greater part of the men were invalids. Certainly, the breakfast was tolerable, but the dinner was often sickening. Such "meat" and "soup" - at least they called it soup. Now that's the worst of some people. They think that by giving a thing a new name they change the substance of it. But it is the easiest matter in the world to be mistaken, and if our stewards thought they could impose a certain aqueous fluid upon us as "soup", which bore as much resemblance to it as bread does to potatoes, they might just as well have whistled the tune of an old ballad. There was one consolation, however, we were on the homeward journey. Once in two days we were paraded for inspection by the officer in charge, at least, all those who were well enough to turn out, and marched about the deck. The weather was fine without interruption. About this time we were all provided with a pair of slippers, a pipe and a cap from the "Absent-minded Beggar" Fund. But there was one thing I did not get which I had coveted very much, and that was the Queen's chocolate. Certainly I had been very near to it. In fact, I had helped to unload it from the vessel when we reached Cape Town on the outward journey, but it was a case of "So near yet so far", and I do not suppose that I shall ever possess it now, or even an empty box. There was no sickness on board this time from the ship's motion, and the men were consequently in the best of spirits. We called at St. Helena and St. Vincent for provisions, etc., where we were visited by the natives, as before, with their fruit baskets. We were much interested in their manners and speech, and they amused us still further by diving for small pieces of money which some of the men threw overboard. The time soon slipped past after we left St. Vincent. Naturally, our approach to England brought a colder atmosphere, and we experienced some rough weather off the Bay of Biscay.

At three o'clock on the morning of November the ninth, we reached the Needles, where we took a pilot, and by ten o'clock we were alongside the jetty, anxiously awaiting to disembark. Several hours passed before we were all ready to leave the ship, but we did so at last, and then we were all dispatched to our destinations.

And now we have reached the end. I hope I have not offended many. It may be that I have interested a few, but to interest and to please are two very different matters. If I have done either in the smallest degree, I shall be both happy and content.

THE END

[This diary was published in 1901 by Morris Brothers of Swindon, the founders of the local evening newspaper which is still in production today.]

Chapter Five

Lord Roberts and Baden Powell
General Kitchener and White
Bravest men of the army
Always ready to fight.

Oh when we get Kruger
How happy we will be
With a flag flying over Pretoria
And Kruger hung in a tree.

(British army song from the Boer War, related to us by Johnny
Morris, O.B.E. as he recalled being sung by his mother.)

We join Nelus through his diary as he prepares to rejoin his
regiment for the South African War, hostilities having been
declared by the Boers on 11th October 1899, after years of
negotiations between them and the British Government. He would
not have been too apprehensive about sailing to war as the
Government were initially sending ten thousand British troops into
South Africa, and confidently expected the Boers to back down at
this show of strength. The whole exercise was expected "to be
over by Christmas." Nelus tells us that he will not go into detail as
to how the Boer War came about as, "of course, everybody is
acquainted with the circumstances which preceded the outbreak",
and hence, in doing so he would be deviating from his personal
task of recounting his own experiences. Today, almost one
hundred years after the outbreak of this, the second Boer War, and
after two world wars and many other subsequent events, the
general public are no longer conversant with the root cause of

these hostilities, so we will try to enlighten the reader with a short summary of the actions and uprisings that led to the South African War.

The Boers, farmers of Dutch origin, had been in South Africa for centuries, and when the British Government had bought the territory from Holland, it was transferred to British rule. This was accepted at first by the Boers, but when the British started to impose laws that took away their autonomy, rebellion started. The abolition of slavery in 1834, part of their national culture, further incensed them. Part of the population accepted conditions under British rule, and became known as Afrikanders, while the remainder decided to migrate to new areas to re-establish their farms. Whole families set out in their ox wagons on a slow trail to found new states for themselves in order to maintain their own independence. This became known as the Great Trek, and those that participated were to become known as Afrikaaners. An attempt to colonise a region and form an independent republic near Durban was short lived when British troops were dispatched to capture the territory, as it encompassed an important harbour vital to the British shipping route to India. Subsequently, the Afrikaaners managed to establish two self-governing states on the high flat lands known as the "veldt". These were sited between the Orange and the Vaal rivers, and were called the "Orange Free State" and the "Transvaal".

The status quo was maintained between the Afrikaaners and the British Government for a short period, until the true wealth of the land started to become evident, firstly with the discovery of diamonds near the Orange river, and then gold was found in the Transvaal. Both of these discoveries attracted many fortune hunters, mainly from Britain, who became known as the "Uitlanders". The expansion of the diamond industry, led by Cecil Rhodes, resulted in the town of Kimberley being built, but the very rapid growth in the mining activities almost caused the State to go bankrupt, and the local African tribes, seizing the moment, started to rebel against their misuse by the British. The Zulus were the largest of these tribes, and under their leader, King Cetewayo, slaughtered a whole column of British troops before being defeated in 1879. A further revolt by the Basuto tribe triggered off another Boer uprising in 1881, which was to become known as the first Boer War of Independence. The main action in this campaign was when the Boers attacked and defeated a strong force of British troops at Majuba Hill, killing the commanding officer, General Colley. Ironically, as Majuba translates as "hill of doves", this particular engagement is remembered in history as a slaughter of British troops, and is referred to by Nelus in his diary on the day of Cronje's surrender as being the anniversary of this particular battle.

Majuba Hill

Official cessation of hostilities was very soon negotiated, but friction between the two sides still continued to exist, and by 1899 trouble had again flared up with the Uitlanders' rebellion against their treatment by the Boers, who were denying them voting rights and equality of pay and conditions. The Uitlanders' grievances were taken up by the British Government, and although some concessions were made by the Boer leader, President Kruger, these were not sufficient, and by the 9th of October all hope of a peace settlement had disappeared, and a state of war was assumed on the 11th October 1899.

President Kruger

Young Boer soldiers

In December 1899, both Nelus and Lord Roberts, representing the lowest and the highest of the army ranks, were each making their own preparations to leave for war.

Lord Roberts

Lord Roberts was born in India in1832, the son of a general, and followed a highly successful army career through all the major campaigns of the mid nineteenth century, culminating as Commander-in-Chief of the British Forces in India, under whom Nelus would have served during his tour of duty there. He was to serve under him again in South Africa, as on February 8th 1900, Lord Roberts arrived at Lord Methuen's camp on the Modder River, having been recalled to service (at the grand age of 67) to take command of the British Forces, and was welcomed by rounds of cheers from the men, who held that "Bobs and luck went hand in hand." He was highly regarded by both the Army and the men, and regarded as "a godsend" by one and all, and it was for this reason that he was asked to take command as the only person that could turn the tide of the War. The Boer War had not got off to a very auspicious start for the British who had woefully underestimated the strength and determination of the Boers and were suffering impending defeat due to under-manning and poor and uninspired leadership. Roberts was seen as the man to pull the army together again, and his decision to take command was strongly influenced by the death of his only son, Lieutenent Frederick Roberts, on December 15th, 1899, was killed whilst engaged in an heroic attempt to save the British guns.

Death of Lieutenant Roberts at Colenso

The strength of his popularity is illustrated by the following account in his biography by Violet Brooke-Hunt which was published in 1901:

These two hundred thousand soldiers needed a leader, and there was one name uppermost in every mind. When the hastily summoned Defence Committee called on Lord Roberts to go out in supreme command with Lord Kitchener as his Chief of Staff, they voiced the desire of the whole nation. It was but a few hours since Roberts had heard the worst from South Africa; that his boy had died of the wounds received at Colenso. 'It is God's will,' he said, as he braced himself for the future.

Nothing but England's claim weighed with him in this hour. Two days before Christmas he sailed. Round Waterloo Station an enormous crowd had gathered to bid him goodbye and God-speed; on the platform itself stood Royal Princes, Cabinet Ministers, with many distinguished soldiers and civilians.

And at the sight of that little white-haired man, with his lined face, and his bright eyes, his well knit upright figure, fresh hope came to the nation.

The crowds cheered him with an intensity of feeling hitherto unknown to the average undemonstrative Englishman, and it was amid this thunder of cheers that the train steamed out of the station: while, in bitter contrast to this send off, of which any man might be justly proud, the newspaper boys in the streets shouted the latest war news, which included one line, 'Burial of Lieutenant Roberts'.

Lieutenant Roberts' grave

Lord Roberts was universally know to his men as "Bobs," and the following is a verse written about him by Rudyard Kipling in 1898:

152

"BOBS"

> "What 'e does not know o' war,
> Gen'ral Bobs,
> You can arst the shop next door-
> Can't they, Bobs?
> Oh 'e's little but 'e's wise,
> 'E's a terror for 'is size,
> An' 'e does not advertise
> Do yer, Bobs?"

The frantic activity that greeted Nelus on his arrival at Cowley would have been mirrored at the various regimental barracks throughout the country, as Britain was to send a grand total of 448,435 men to war in South Africa by the end of the campaign. Telegrams and donations for the men were pouring in from all parts of the country, and patriotism and optimism were riding hide, as evidenced by the following communications received at Cowley Barracks:

"Good luck to you and a safe return. - 4th Rifle Brigade."

"Best congratulations on departure for South Africa; hope Regiment will have many opportunities of increasing brilliant record, and all return safe and well. - Payne, 15 Alva Street, Edinburgh."

"Hope you will kindly inform me when Regiment starts for seat of war, as I should like to send the men pipes and tobacco. I wish the Regiment every success in South Africa. - Rothschild, New Court."

This letter is from Field-Marshall Lord Roberts to the Commanding Officer:-

"Allow me to congratulate you most heartily on getting command of the Battalion at such an opportune time, and please let all ranks know how glad I am that they have been selected for service. I feel sure they will worthily uphold the glorious traditions of the Old 43rd Light Infantry."

An old 43rd Officer sent a cheque for £50, many others sent smaller amounts, but the most remarkable gift was one of twenty guineas from Mr H.C.Lea, formerly of the Ox & Bucks, who with the cheque wrote: "It affords me great satisfaction to think that I am able to give my old Regiment something before it leaves for South Africa."

In all, nearly £200 was received, and put into a Commanding Officer's fund for the purpose of assisting the men during the campaign. Nelus records in his diary that on his voyage home he received a pair of slippers, a pipe and a cap from the "Absent-Minded Beggar Fund" - this could well have been the nickname for the above collection, and perhaps made up a little for him having missed out on the Queen's chocolate!

A good deal of pomp and ceremony was involved with the departure of the Regiment to war, as evidenced by this contemporary account of the depositing of the Regimental Colours in the Cathedral for safekeeping, which appeared in the Times on the 11th December 1899.

The Colours at Oxford Cathedral

The Oxfordshire Light Infantry Colours

An impressive service was held in Christ Church Cathedral, Oxford on Saturday afternoon, on the occasion of depositing the Regimental Colours of the Oxfordshire Light Infantry within the cathedral, where they will remain whilst the Regiment is on active service in South Africa. The colours were conveyed from Aldershot by an escort consisting of Captain Watt and Lieutenants, the Hon.G.W.Foljambe and A.G.Bayley, three colour sergeants and about twenty rank and file. At Oxford Railway Station the Non-Commissioned Officers and men fixed bayonets, and with the colours flying, borne by the two lieutenants, they marched to the Cathedral, the men being greeted with repeated cheering throughout the route by the crowds which lined the streets. The Cathedral was thronged. Amongst those present were the Vice-Chancellor (the President of Corpus Christi) and many distinguished members of the University, Lord Valentia, M.P., Mr.G.H.Morrell, M.P., Sir Henry Acland, the Bishop of Reading, the Rev.Canons Ince, Bright, Moberly, Sanday and Driver. The Mayor and members of the Corporation, attired in their scarlet robes, walked in procession to the Cathedral. The colour-bearers advanced to the chancel steps with the colour-sergeants, and the rank and file of the escorts marched up the aisle and stood with fixed bayonets two deep behind the colours. The service commenced with the singing of the Old Hundredth Hymn. The Colours were received by the Dean of Christ Church (Dr. Paget), who, standing on the chancel steps and holding a colour in each hand, said he thankfully accepted the trust with which the Regiment had honoured them. The Colours should be kept in the Cathedral with honour and reverence until they returned, please God, in safety - and God grant it might be ere long - to reclaim them. Meanwhile the Colours would not be idle or without meaning, for they would know that they were there and guarded in this house of God and reverenced by them as by the Regiment. And they would be a constant help, helping them to make their prayers for the men very constant and very earnest, and helping also to keep before them the standard of duty and obedience and courage and soldierly loyalty, which was the secret of an honourable life, whether it be for soldiers or for civilians. He bade the men present and those they represented goodbye and god-speed. They were going to serve a Queen who loved her people and had never failed to do her utmost for their welfare and happiness. They were going to serve a country dear, most dear, to them, and of which they were all proud - a country that had ever held high the standard of honour and liberty and justice. God grant to them all to live day by day that they might not be afraid, if it be His will to die, or to live that the fear of death might, please God, seem as

nothing to them in comparison with the sense of duty. God be with them
now and always. They all were in His hands, and might He in His love
and mercy help them all according to their several callings to do His
will. The short service was brought to a conclusion with the singing of
the National Anthem, in which the large congregation heartily joined.

The S.S.Gaika that took Nelus to South Africa belonged to the
Union Company, and was a passenger ship hired by the Army. As
well as his Regiment, which comprised of 660 men of all ranks,
there were also 881 men of the 2nd Battalion East Kent Regiment
(the Buffs) and a few private passengers who were dropped off at
Tenerife to spend the winter at Orotava for health reasons. The
complement was completed by four men of the 13th Brigade staff
(including Major-General Knox), four of Post Office Corps, ten
Military Foot Police, and fifty seven men of No.7 Company
R.A.M.C. as well as three Warrant Officers and nine horses. As
the ship sailed off to war, with the band of the "Buffs" playing on
board, the Gaika was sent on its way to the cheers of the old
officers and non-commissioned officers who were lining the
harbour, and had come down especially to see them go. The
Oxford Times bid them farewell with the thoughts of those they
left behind, with this verse:

AT DUTY'S CALL

Good-bye, ye Oxford Redcoats!
You're wanted far away;
And may your bearing ever be
As gallant as today.

You know we wouldn't lose you-
We bid you to be gone
Because Old England needs your arms;
So onward, Oxford! On!

May health and safety cheer you
While riding on the waves,
And land you safe in Table Bay
Among good Buller's braves.

May fortune star attend you
And guide you in the fight-
We know you'll stand up gallantly
And battle for the right.

Although the snow is falling,
And wintry is the scene,
Your hearts are warmly beating for
Your country and your Queen.

They say you're "absent-minded"-
But, be it false or true,
Old Oxford will remember, and
Her heart will be with you.

And now away, ye Redcoats,
To Afric's sunny shores-
From Oxford to Pretoria,
To tame the boasting Boers.

They're coming, "Uncle" Kruger!
You'll soon be hearing from
The men who left their battle-flag
Beneath Old Oxford Tom.

Once Nelus' ship had set sail, and all the pomp and ceremony had died down, he would have had ample chance to consider the dangers that lay ahead, and to wonder if he would ever see England and his home again that he had seen so little of over the last eight years. The wrench of leaving home yet again would have been strengthened by the fact that it was Christmas in three days' time, and although he enjoyed a special lunch on board, his thoughts were still with those he had left at home.

New year's eve is normally a time for celebration and optimism for the fresh year to come, but the dawning of a whole new century, not to be experienced in everybody's lifetime, should bring an extra special celebration. However, the general mood of the Nation at the end of 1899 was far too apprehensive to make much of this occasion, for the Country was at war again, and the majority of families had at least one loved one, a husband, father, brother, son or sweetheart, thousands of miles away at the front in South Africa. A small contemporary booklet entitled "Peace" sums up the mood of the time thus:- "Deep was the gloom in which the Old Year passed away, and dark and stormy was the dawn of 1900." In his diary, Nelus makes no mention of any new year's eve festivities at all on board his ship, just "Tea as usual", and "retire", and New Year's Day is only marked by "turning over a new leaf" and a game of "House" in the afternoon.

Various games were played by those on board to relieve the monotony of the long voyage, although sometimes the answers given by the contestants were a little dubious, as is illustrated in an account by Vincent Low, a surgeon, on his way to South Africa aboard the Kinfauns Castle on January 18th, 1900, a month after Nelus had sailed:

There were competitive races, and men and women rushed to and fro with various difficult problems to solve, struggling to reach the judge first with their answers. To the question "How many hams have forty pigs?" the answer "80" was almost unanimous. To everyone's astonishment, Captain Merrilees, the judge, disagreed, and affirmed that "160" was the correct solution.

This judgement became the topic of much discussion thereafter, to the extent that Rudyard Kipling, who happened to be aboard, penned this humerous verse on Vincent's program of events:

> The World was made in seven days
> By God, the Great Designer
> Who gave each pig two hams apiece,
> Save on a Castle liner-
> Save in the Kinfauns Castle sports
> As judged by Merrilees,
> When every little porker has
> As many as you please.

Game of cricket on board ship

On the 9th January, Nelus mentions illness on board affecting both the men and the horses, which he puts down to sea-sickness, due to them hitting rough weather after the calm of the previous two weeks. This was not the only health worry, as influenza was also rife on board at the time, causing some fatalities. Among the equine casualties were the chargers of Major Pike on the 8th, and General Knox on the 9th, which caused difficulties with the disposal of their carcasses at sea. This problem was compounded on a subsequent voyage when the Mounted Infantry Companies of the 6th Division of the Ox and Bucks sailed with 480 horses on board the Pindari three weeks later. Not only were there far more preparations required, with all the horses' tackle to pack and load in addition to the usual tents, blankets and kit of the men, but the logistics of their care must have taken a great deal of effort and planning.

Except when the weather was too rough, every horse was taken out of its box and groomed daily, which proved so time consuming that physical drill for the men was practically dispensed with. We can imagine what a hive of activity this ship must have been with all these animals on board, especially after weeks at sea, when they would have been becoming restless after the long period of confinement without exercise. No doubt Nelus' crossing would have seemed like a pleasure cruise compared to

159

the frantic activity of the voyage to South Africa for the mounted brigades. During their crossing, 23 horses died and had to be buried at sea; nevertheless, when the Pindari docked at Cape Town, she had the second-best average for horse ships from England. It took 6 hours to disembark on arrival, and the horses were then taken to Maitland Camp, where they were turned loose into wire kraals, and due to their long period of confinement, it proved very difficult to prevent them from breaking out, some running clean over the wire and injuring themselves so badly that they had to be shot.

Stabling on board ship

Injured horse being shot

Further problems were encountered later when most of the men had to be actually taught to ride, a sight that would probably have brought a smile to the faces of any Boers who may have happened to be looking on.

On February 13th, the Mounted Section of this Company left by train to join up with Nelus' part of the Regiment. The scene on mounting when leaving Maitland Camp for Cape Town Station was most amusing, "Men mounting from the nearside; mounting from the offside; men lying on their backs on the ground; men with their arms round their horses necks, and the horses kicking and squealing all over the field." Once entrained, the problems did not end as, with more than twenty horses placed in most of the trucks, one or two were continually falling down and the train had to keep stopping at stations to put them back on their feet.

All mounted!

Nelus mentions the decline in standard of the rations after he has disembarked from the Gaika, at a time when the Boers appear to have enjoyed a better diet. When the Mounted Infantry stumbled upon a farm at Jasfontein where the Boers had stayed, sardine tins were especially noticeable, no doubt making our men's mouths water, as they were surviving on a small daily ration of dried biscuits. Their supplies had been recently hit when a train carrying three days supplies for the whole force had overturned a mile from Rensburg Station, and a detachment had to be sent to burn the train, to prevent the provisions falling into enemy hands. General Clements, in command of this group, was amused to notice on one of the doors at the station, a Boer had written the following:

"Question. - How many kinds of fools are there?

161

Answer. - Three. The fool; the ------fool; and the British General."

Shortly after, Lord Roberts arrived at the Modder River to discover the chronic shortage of supplies following the overturned train, and summoned the head of the Army Service department, and asked him whether he could guarantee full supplies during the forthcoming movement that he was planning:

"I cannot, Sir," was the answer.

"Three-quarter rations?"

"No, Sir."

"Half? "

"I cannot answer for it."

"Quarter-rations?"

"Yes, Sir."

"Well," said Lord Roberts, "I think they will do it for me," and he was right! As the monthly news magazine of the time, "With the Flag to Pretoria" observes, "a less determined, a less beloved general, might well have shrunk from running so immense a risk or from laying so terrible a burden upon the physique and endurance of his men."

Near Thebus, where Nelus and his Regiment were helping with the repair of a railway bridge destroyed by the enemy, the darker side of the Boers' nature was observed. An officer reports that:

We saw a most revolting sight at one of the farms here yesterday, - a deaf and dumb idiot chained up to a post in front of the house. The poor creature was filthy dirty, and apparently treated like a dog. From all accounts idiots are very numerous in the country, and they are always treated in this way; they are supposed to be the result of the in-breeding among the Dutch farmers.

Throughout his diary, Nelus expresses the patriotism, energy and enthusiasm for the task in hand shown by himself and his comrades in the Regiments, and this is illustrated by a report written at the time by one of the officers:

The marching of the infantry, considering the great heat and the absence of water, once more proves that the British soldier is willing and ready to respond to any call. The men never faltered. Some fell out of the ranks from sheer exhaustion; but these, as soon as they had sufficiently recovered, seized the first opportunity to rejoin their Companies. It was, perhaps, a finer sight than any battle to see the Battalions moving through the heavy sand under a broiling sun, every man determined, persevering, and cheerful. Not a murmur was heard, and the whole force was animated by a grand faith in their Commander. It is no exaggeration to say that nearly the whole of the troops, horse, foot, and artillery, and especially the transport service men, had not more than three hours' sleep on any of the last three nights. Yet there is no sign of any falling off in their health or strength. All are willing and cheerful, and ready and anxious to do all that men can do.

Major Caunter D.A.A.G, of the Sixth Division of the Regiment reports the following incident:

After Klip Kraal fight, I came across a wounded man of the Oxfordshire Light Infantry, and inquired about his wounds and condition. His reply was in the form of a question as to how the Regiment had behaved in action - showing that the uppermost thought in a soldier's mind was the well-being of his Corps.

The soldiers appeared to take the risks of war, with its possibility of instant death or injury, all in their stride. Nelus states on the 29th January, in a most deadpan fashion, how a couple of hours' skirmishing in the morning "put new life in us," and then goes on to tell the reader how he washed his shirt and socks in the afternoon, and spread them out to dry. He almost seems oblivious of the very real danger that the morning's fighting entailed, and covers the fact that he fortunately survived being killed or wounded by occupying his narrative with the most mundane of actions. This could have been because, after years of action on front-lines, the risk of injury had become "old hat", and no longer deemed worthy of consideration, or that the fear of action and possible sudden death was masked in the emotions by everyday chores to help preserve his sanity and calm his nerves. Their lighthearted attitude towards danger is again illustrated in an extract from a letter by a Lieut.-Colonel, The Hon.A.E.Dalzell of the Regiment, who describes an incident prior to the Battle of Paardeberg:

Lieutenant-Colonel The Hon. A.E.Dalzell

It was quite early in the morning when we advanced against the Boers, composed of from 2-3000 of Cronje's men, and we were the Right Regiment of the Brigade, having the river on our right. Lord Kitchener was very anxious to get some men across the river, but it was supposed to be impassable, as the enemy held a very strong position along its bank (at the bend which ran along our right flank, about a mile in front,) from which they were already peppering us; Knox, our Brigadier, came up to me, and said, 'I'm afraid it's no good, but if you could get over the river anyhow we might best them.' I ran along the bank, searching keenly for some possible place, and had at last determined to try and swim the Regiment over. Porter (an officer) tried at one place, sank up to his armpits in the muddy bottom, and convulsed me with laughter. Suddenly, I saw a rock protruding from our bank, which I argued, probably pointed to a bit of rocky bed, and so it proved, enabling us all to wade across, up to our middles only. I sent word back to Lord Kitchener that we were across, and that I should advance at once unless he ordered otherwise. When we were all over (Stapleton got his Maxim across very cleverly,) I extended two Companies across the open country, as a blind, whilst I sent three Companies up the river bank amongst the trees and bushes, Porter and I running backwards and forwards to encourage the men, the fire by this time having become fast and furious. Porter and I both very nearly got bagged here, and I felt quite sorry for Porter on one occasion when a bullet missed me by a hair, throwing up all the dirt into my mouth as we lay side by side in the open. Porter said, 'Hullo! Colonel!' as if he had almost felt the promotion in his grasp!

Two further incidents of this nature were reported in the magazine "With the Flag to Pretoria":

Doctor Stark, a British doctor who believed the War was unjust, had come to Ladysmith to tend the Boer wounded who fell into our hands. He always took shelter in the caves, but the shells seemed to pursue him. The Boers usually ceased firing in the evening, and one night he had come back to the hotel, after what he had supposed the last gun, when several rounds were rapidly fired from the six inch Creusot on Lombard's Kop. A shot actually struck him just as he reached the door of the hotel, and inflicted upon him such terrible injuries that he died almost at once. A kitten which he always carried with him to his cave in a basket, that the poor little creature might be safe, was unharmed. His last unselfish words as he lay dying were, 'Take care of my cat.'

A sergeant of the Liverpools who left his shelter out of curiosity just after a shell had burst, was caught by another projectile and torn almost to pieces. As they lifted him back to the shelter he only said, 'Wasn't it a pity I went out to see it?'

Taking a gun across the River Modder at Paardeberg

However, the enthusiasm of the Boers for action was not always so strong, especially in the preceding days to the battle of Paardeberg, when their leader Cronje was under heavy pressure from some of his men to surrender, as they could see their position weakening daily. One of the deserters from the Boers who made his way to the British lines told them that the previous day's bombardment was "deadly and terrible in its effects:- the howitzers especially, battering the river bed with an enfilading fire." A British doctor visiting the Boer lines at this time found the trenches near the river full of wounded, and saw many dead. Frequent marks of blood showed where the wounded and dead had been removed from where they had fallen; the Boer method for removal of the dead was to tie two reigns around the body, which is then dragged off at full gallop by horsemen.

Nelus gives a most descriptive account of the action and the full horror of the pivotal battle of Paardeberg, and General Piet Cronje's subsequent surrender. On February 18th, he records the heavy fighting of that day with many killed and wounded, including Major-General Knox amongst the latter. One of the fatalities which Nelus omits to mention was Major Charles Russell Day who had served with him in India and sailed with him to South Africa aboard the S.S.Gaika; the news of his death had obviously not reached him before he wrote up his diary. Major Day had a most unfortunate death, having survived two near misses in the preceding two days; on the 16th he was caught in heavy fire at Klip Kraal and whilst lying on the ground his field-glasses were smashed to pieces by a bullet; at Paardeberg on the 18th he was severely, though not dangerously injured, and would most probably have recovered, but while he was being carried from the field of combat, he was hit a second time by an explosive bullet, the result of which proved fatal two days later. His funeral on the 21st February was described by the Chaplin as the most impressive one at which he had ever officiated: "Major-General Knox, himself severely wounded, attended, and although the Regiment, being at the time in action, was unable to be present, twenty or thirty of the wounded men from the hospital managed to find their way to the graveside, to show their respect for their officer."

The Church Times of April 6th 1900, published a letter regarding Major Day's funeral from the Rev. J.Blackburn, Chaplin to the Forces, from which the following is an extract:

On February 21st, I buried Major Day, of the Oxfordshire Light Infantry. It was a most pathetic funeral. About thirty wounded men of his Regiment and General Knox followed. These men were wounded in every conceivable part of the body; they made a sad picture as we wended our way to the grave. Not many of us returned with dry eyes.

Major Day was the only son of the Reverend Russell Day, Rector of Horstead, Norfolk, and Maria Isabella, eldest daughter T.J.Knowlys Esquire of Haeysham Tower, Lancashire, and was born on the 19th April, 1860. He was educated at Cheam School and Eton.

Major Day

The most important event that Nelus was involved in during his experiences in South Africa was the battle of Paaderberg, and the surrender of General Cronje, one of the main Boer leaders, which he graphically describes in his diary. Another contemporary account recreates for us some of the horrors that Nelus thought better to omit, and the full pathos of Cronje's surrender:

. . .Still, the Boers were kept crouching in their trenches, and were condemned to watch their wagons one by one catching fire and burning to ashes. What horses and cattle in the laager had not been killed in the previous bombardments perished in this, and the interior of the laager became a horrible mass of putrefying carcasses, the stench of which poisoned the air for miles. The water in the river was so low that it would not carry off the bodies, and there was no where to bury them. So foul was the horrible fluid which the river yielded that it came to be known among our men as "Dead Horse Soup"....

Cronje's laager

.....First word of Cronje's surrender was brought in by two Boer officers, riding horses that had been slightly wounded by the British shrapnel fire, almost the last horses left in the laager. Cronje, the determined, the indomitable, had been compelled to yield before the clamour of his men, who dreaded the awful slaughter of the bayonet assault, which they saw impending. A message was sent back from the British Commander-in-Chief requesting the Boer general to make his surrender in person to Lord Roberts. General Pretyman and a small escort rode out to meet the stubborn soldier of Modder River and Magersfontein. The momentous scene at Lord Roberts headquarters is thus described by a brilliant eye witness, a Mr Hands:- 'The trim figure of the Chief caught my eye first. He was alone in front of the little lean-to tent fixed to the side of a travelling wagon in which he works and sleeps. His grey face, grave and thoughtful, showed no sign of elation. He looked around, gave an order

*to one of his staff, and a table and two chairs were brought out of his
tent and placed under the shade of a tree at the edge of the riverbank. He
gave another order, and half a company of Highlanders formed up in
three sides of a square about the spot. The Chief looked carefully
around, saw that everything was in order, then walked to his tent. When
he came out again, he was wearing his sword - a heavy sword with a
jewelled hilt. It was the first time I had seen him wearing it since the
column started. But he forgets nothing, overlooks nothing, considers
everything. And he had donned his sword now as a mark of respect for
his fallen foe.*

Lord Roberts' headquarters at Paardeberg

*Presently the body of horsemen came past the hospital tents into the
camp. Major-General Pretyman was one of the leading horsemen, his
compact figure lightly swinging with the movement of his charger. By his
side a great heavy bundle of a man was lumped atop of a wretched little
grey boney war pony. And this was the terrible Cronje. Was it possible
that this was the man who had held back the British Army at
Magersfontein? Great square shoulders, from which the heavy head was
thrust forward so that he seemed almost humped; a heavy face, shapeless
with unkempt, grey-tinged, black hair; lowering heavy brows, from under
which small, cunning, foxy eyes peered shiftily. A broad-brimmed grey
Boer felt hat was pulled down low, a loose brown overcoat, ordinary
dark trousers; nothing military, not even spurs on his brown veldt boots.
The only thing he carried that seemed to speak authority was his
sjambok, a thick heavy stocked whip of hide, which he grasped and*

swung as one accustomed to use it. With Cronje rode a lean and spectacled interpreter; for though the Boer General spoke English perfectly, it suited him to pretend that he knew only Dutch. Lord Roberts stepped forward, saluted, shook hands, and handed his fallen enemy a chair. The two sat down and fell to quiet, unemotional talk.

General Cronje surrenders to Lord Roberts

'I am glad to see you; I am glad to meet so brave a man,' was Lord Roberts' welcome to his foe.

Cronje's face was set and sullen. Few, perhaps, of the correspondents and officers who stood watching that historic meeting realised the agony of heart which this moment of surrender meant for the Boer. His shabby attire suggested the tramp rather than the soldier, yet in its very uncouth simplicity there was pathos. As he looked forth beyond the guard of motionless Highlanders, he saw the thousands upon thousands of British soldiers, their cannon, their countless transport wagons, and all their elaborate apparatus of war. He knew that this was the first occasion in the campaign upon which a perfectly equipped force had entered the field under a leader of genius. Behind the tragedy of his personal defeat, and overshadowing it, was the yet greater tragedy of his country's downfall. He averted his eyes steadily from his conqueror until at last the painful meeting terminated. Lord Roberts rose, bowed, and retired, and Cronje was left to the staff.

From the dispatches of Lord Roberts we have the transcript of Cronje's letter of surrender, received at 6.00 a.m. on the 27th February:-

Headquarter Laager, Modder River
27th February, 1900.

HONOURED SIR, --- *Herewith I have the honour to inform you that the Council of War, which was held here last evening, resolved to surrender unconditionally with the forces here, being compelled to do so under existing circumstances. They therefore throw themselves on the clemency of Her Britannic Majesty.*

As a sign of surrender a white flag will be hoisted from 6.00 am today. The Council of War requests that you will give immediate orders for all further hostilities to be stopped, in order that more loss of life may be prevented.

> *I have the honour to be, Sir,*
> *Your most obedient servant,*
> *(Signed) P.A.CRONJE, General*

On receipt of this letter, Lord Roberts, advised High Command back in England of the surrender, by the following telegraphic despatch sent at 7.45.a.m. that day from Paardeberg:

General Cronje and all his force capitulated unconditionally at daylight this morning, and is now a prisoner in my camp. The strength of his force will be communicated later. I hope Her Majesty's Government will consider this event satisfactory, occurring as it does on the anniversary of Majuba.

(The battle of Majuba took place on British Territory just inside the borders of Natal, on Sunday, 27th February 1881, when General Sir George Pomeroy Colley, Govenor of Natal and South-East Africa, and four hundred men lost their lives.)

At 11.00 a.m. Lord Roberts sent a further message part of which we reproduce here:

This apparently clinched matters, for at daylight today, a letter signed by Cronje, in which he stated that he surrendered unconditionally, was brought to our outposts under the flag of truce.

In my reply, I told Cronje that he must present himself at my camp, and that his force must come out of their laager after laying down their arms. By 7.00 a.m. I received General Cronje, and dispatched a telegram to

171

you announcing the fact. In the course of conversation he asked for kind treatment at our hands, and also that his wife, grandson, private secretary, adjutant, and servants might accompany him wherever he might be sent. I reassured him, and told him his request would be complied with. I informed him that a General Officer would be sent with him to Cape Town to ensure his being treated with proper respect en route. He will start this afternoon under the charge of Major-General Pretyman, who will hand him over to the General Commanding at Cape Town. The prisoners, who number about three thousand, will be formed into commandos under their own officers. They will also leave here today, reaching Modder River tomorrow, when they will be railed to Cape Town in detachments.

A continuing telegraph was sent at 1.05 p.m.

Boer prisoners amount to about four thousand, of whom one thousand one hundred and fifty are Free Staters, the remainder Transvaalers. The officers are as follows:-

Transvaalers

General Piet Cronje.
Chief Commandant M.J.Wolverans.
Commandants F.J.Roos, J.T.Maartens.
Assistant Commandants R.Woest and J.P.G.Verster.
Camp Commandant W.L.Joost.
Field Cornets Alberts and Vande, JH.L.Bosman, W.A.Lemmer, H.J.Badenhorst, Frus (Who is a Scandinavian), D.H.Hattings, and Venter D.J.Terblanche.
Acting Field Cornets P.V.De Villiers, G.J.Du Plessis.
Assistant Field Cornet. R.J. Sneyman.
War Commissioner Arnoldi.
Assistant War Commissioner B.J.Joost.
Magazine Master A.K.Enslin.
Adjutants J.M.A.Wolverans, A.D.W.R.Jolverans, A.Uing, M.S.Maree, J.A.Botha, and G.H.Grobler, in charge of Artillery.
Farrier Thomas Moodie.

Free Staters.

Commandants J.P.Wordaan, J.K.Kok, J.C.Villiers, R.J.Sneyman, S.Meintjes, J.Greyling, Smith.

Field Cornets J.Cronje, C.Oosthuisen, C.Van Lyl, J.Nieuvenhal, M.Kvick, J.Kvick, J.Van der Walt.
Commandant of Artillery, Major Albrecht.
Lieutenants Vaen-Heister, Van Dewitz, Van Angersteins.
Guns captured are as follows:- From Transvaal - three 7.5 centimetre Krupp 9-pounders and one Maxim. From Orange Free State - one 7.5 centimetre Krupp, one Maxim.

The Boer War was only the latest in a series of conflicts in the area ranging back over the years, and, as always, the soldiers involved respected the memories of those who had fought before: the Regimental Journal gives us this account of when Nelus' Regiment reached Bloemfontein shortly after he had left for hospital with the other sick and wounded from the battle:

We discovered in the cemetery here the other day, the grave of a 43rd soldier who died of wounds during the Kaffir War. The stone, like many others, has evidently been used as a target by the Boers at musketry practice in the old fort (some seven hundred yards away), but it was still in fair preservation, and the surrounding ground and the mound were soon put in order by willing hands. The following is the inscription on the stone:-

Sacred to the Memory of
JOHN DELAP,
Late of H.M.'s 43Rd Regiment
Light Infantry,
Who died from wounds received in
Action, on 28th day of December 1852,
Aged 27 years.

This Tablet was erected by the Detachment
45th Regiment, as a token of respect to a
Brother Soldier.

Even 48 years later, and in a different war, the dead soldier was still treated as one of their own, and his grave tended accordingly.

Although Nelus spent two days in the Orange River Hospital in what he describes as "ease and comfort", his opinion of the conditions would have been heavily influenced by the extreme medical staff were in very short supply, it was often left to soldiers to double up as orderlies, and even administer treatment at times. The limited resources of these hospitals was stretched to the limits by an epidemic of enteric fever which was caused by the drinking of tainted water from the river at Paardeberg, heavily polluted by the corpses of men and animals; instructions had been issued to boil all water before drinking, but the men, desperate to slake their thirst after the battle, largely ignored these instructions with disastrous consequences. Within a few days, a thousand men were in hospital suffering from the fever, and this number rapidly quadrupled, until, by the end of April there were four thousand five hundred patients in Bloemfontein, and thousands more, as Nelus was, transported on to their hospitals in the Cape Colony. Seventy five out of every thousand soldiers ended up in hospital at this time, and out of the two hundred thousand troops then in South Africa, fifteen thousand were in hospital. Casualties of these proportions would strain the resources of even the most modern equipped hospitals of today, let alone the primitive establishments then in use. The scale of this epidemic seriously affected Lord Roberts' campaign, as he was forced to delay further progress for seven weeks.

Vincent Warren Low, a surgeon in the field hospital at the battle of Paardeberg, describes the chronic conditions he had to work under during the action of 21st February, 1900:

Since I left Modder River it has been nothing but fighting and marching; we have marched day and night; everyone has been thoroughly worn out, with only half-rations of food, and two or three times I have had nothing but muddy water for twenty four hours on end. We had a dickens of a battle on Sunday, and in fact it is not over yet, as Cronje surrendered but afterwards backed out of it; however, I believe we have him on toast here. Our hospital got under fire, both shell and rifle, and we had to put nearly sixty wounded out of the fire zone. However, we didn't lose anybody except our water-cart mules, but had to leave all our tents behind us, and I shall never forget that night on the veldt; we bivouacked between the lines (Boers and ours - though we did not know it at the time) without any shelter, with about sixty wounded men and no water or food. However, we are fairly comfortable at present, and not under fire, which is a change. I don't know how I have got through the last three days. From sunrise to late at night I have been dressing and operating; they give me all the surgery, and I do just as I like, but it is fearful; some of the wounds are appalling, and these cursed dust-storms cover wounds and everything with about an inch of dust. I am glad you can't see me, as my face is all blistered by the sun, I haven't shaved for ten days, I am reduced to one shirt which is black, and I have given all my others to poor beggars who are wounded and haven't a stitch. I wash about once in two days, and a bath once in three days is luxurious. I haven't seen bread since I left Modder, and ration biscuit reminds me of Spratts! Otherwise we live on bully beef and goat killed about half an hour before use; the water is a thick yellow, and there is no time to filter it, and all our food is accompanied by large portions of dust. I don't suppose it is possible to be more uncomfortable, as we sleep in our clothes on the ground and it is jolly cold at night, and one wakes in the morning worse in the matter of dust and dirt than Tommy Atkins at his utmost. However, I would not have missed it for worlds, and shall stick it for the rest of the campaign.

Field hospital at Paardeberg

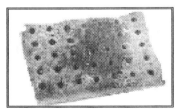

Army ration biscuit

Field surgeon at work

He continues:

I took Bobs (Lord Roberts) round the hospital, and can understand why he is so popular. It is no particular fun here, as we sleep in the open, all the tents being wanted for the wounded, and there is a thunder storm every night; we are also on half-rations as the Boers have destroyed a big supply convoy, the river is within a hundred yards of our camp, and this morning I counted forty dead horses and cattle float by, and that is not counting what are sticking in the trees at the side, consequently the atmosphere is not worth mentioning. Anybody found looting is going to be hanged, and his regiment sent to the base, consequently we all turn pale at the sight of a fowl in case we might be tempted!

Vincent Low was a demonstrator of anatomy, and struggling to make ends meet, when he got a letter from the War Office on January 5th, 1900, offering him a post as surgeon attached to Number 6 General Hospital in South Africa, a position he was delighted to accept. He later went on to practice in Harley Street.

News of the unsatisfactory hospital conditions filtered back to England, and the Times newspaper sent Mr W. Burdett-Coutts, M.P. to South Africa to report on the medical and hospital arrangements there for the troops. This produced an alarming picture of medical neglect, and it was considered that in this war, as in the Crimean, the Government and the War Office had again failed to prepare adequate facilities to safeguard the health of the troops. Following pressure from the press, a Royal Commission was appointed by the Government to report on the care of the sick and wounded during the War, and, as a result, conditions gradually improved.

On Friday March 22nd, 1901, just under a month after Cronje's surrender at Paardeberg, The Swindon Advertiser, Nelus' home-town newspaper and the publisher of his diary, printed a stirring poem sent home by Bandsman W.H.Thorne of 1st Oxfordshire Light Infantry (Nelus' regiment) and very probably a relation through his half-brother William Thorne.

War! War! What hast though done for me,
And thousands more besides,
Who've had to leave their dear old homes,
Their children and their wives?

Some are not wed, but good homes had,
With a mother kind and dear;
While others have a good old dad
Who's shed many a bitter tear.

But we have left our homes to fight.
For our Queen and Country dear,
And when we've put the foe to flight,
We'll return with all good cheer.

We are fighting for our country's rights,
And by God's help we'll win;
For every British soldier fights,
And never will give in.

We fought the Boers at Klip Kraal Drift,
We drove them from the hills,
We followed them to Paardeberg
Where was broke their stubborn wills.

We fought throughout the Sabbath day,
With neither food or drink,
And who did to the river stray
Were shot upon its brink.

That day of days, most dreadful day,
Of pain and death all round;
Wounded and killed I saw them lay
Like sheep upon the ground.

I heard the wounded's pitious cry
For water for their lips:
But every bottle was quite dry
Not one man had two sips.

Our wounded were about two score,
With about a dozen killed:
Some good old pals we'll see no more
For a warrior's grave they've filled.

We still fought on, ten days or more,
And got them well in hand;
We had Cronje and his thousand four,
For he had made his last brave stand.

Now fighting o'er at Paardeberg,
We marched to Osfontein,
Where we took a little hard-earned rest,
And then marched on again.

We marched by night, as well as day,
On biscuits numbering two;
And on the veldt we often lay,
With no blankets, in the dew.

We often marched with water nil,
And empty stomachs too;
But we did our duty with a will
That becomes a soldier true.

178

We followed to Bloemfontein,
The Orange Free State city,
Where Kruger and his comrade Steyn,
Their troops did try to rally.

But no, they did not take the pill,
They did not want our physic;
They would not stay to try the steel
Or even smell the lyddite.

Of course some tradesmen stayed at home,
And well they let us know it;
Their prices nearly struck us numb,
But of course we had to buy it.

Sugar at two bob per pound,
Sixpence for a cup of tea;
In the town and all around
It's daylight robbery.

Fresh butter's cheap at three and six,
At least that's what they say,
For loaves of bread as hard as bricks,
A bob we have to pay.

But when the war is once all o'er,
We'll return to Old England again;
Back to the land we love once more,
None the worse for our hard campaign.

Bandsman W.H.Thorne
1st Oxfordshire Light Infantry
Field Force, South Africa.

For his tour of duty in the Boer War, Nelus was awarded the Queen's Medal with the Relief of Kimberley and Battle of Paardeberg clasps. The clasp inscribed: "Relief of Kimberley" was granted to all troops in the relief column under Lieut-Gen French, who marched from Klip Drift on 15th Febrary, 1900, and all the 6th Division under Lieut-Gen. Kelly-Kenny who were within 7000 yards of Klip Drift on 15th February, 1900. The Paardeberg clasp was granted to all troops within 7000 yards of General Cronje's final laager, between midnight of the 17th and midnight of the 26th February, 1900, and to all troops within 7000 yards of Koodoe's Rand Drift between those dates.

Soldiers looting a Boer farmhouse prior to burning it

Boer women trying to salvage possessions
before their home is burnt

The British were remembered after the war for two types of "atrocities", Lord Roberts' burn and destroy policy, and the invention of concentration camps. Under the former, Lord Roberts' orders were that when the army came upon a Boer farmhouse, if the man of the house was not present, it was assumed that he was fighting the British, as was often the case. The remaining family, consisting of women, young children and the elderly, were then given five minutes to remove what possessions they could, and then they could only huddle together in fright and watch as their remaining furniture and livestock was looted by the soldiers, and the farmstead set on fire.

Boer farmhouse being burnt

News of the terrible consequences of the burning of the farmsteads spread rapidly, and the outcry was so great that Lord Roberts issued orders that it must stop, unless an officer deemed it necessary; unfortunately, most of the time this appeared to be the case, as the looting of the livestock provided the soldiers with a welcome feast to supplement their often monotonous diet. Ironically, any theft of livestock or other food by the often starving black Africans was looked on with the utmost severity by the British, and was often punishable by death.

The dispossessed families often wandered off into the veldt, where many met their deaths from exposure, starvation or attacks from hostile tribes. Because of the high mortality of the Boer families, as a direct result of the farm burning policy, the British Government decided that it must take responsibility for them, and instructions were issued for them to be taken to "points of concentration" near the railways, where camps were built to house them. Both the Boers and the black Africans were treated in this way, but usually housed in separate camps.

On trial for his life for stealing a goat

Boer women being taken to a concentration camp

Initially these concentration camps were constructed of wooden huts, but as numbers rapidly increased, the accommodation was reduced to rows of bell tents. As many of the refugees as possible were found work to do, for which they were paid a small remuneration, but as conditions worsened, their time was taken up more and more with nursing their sick and dying. Their food was rationed, and the medical authorities, with the dietary ignorance of the time, considered fresh vegetables unnecessary to a healthy diet, so reducing their staple rations to tins of bully beef imported from America, with the resultant lowering of their immune system. This led to them being unable to fight off the normal childhood diseases which became epidemic within the cramped conditions of the camps, and combined with the cold of the extreme winters, led to thousands of deaths.

A concentration camp

A written account from a Boer mother Alie Badenhorst, an inmate of one of these camps, describes the horrific consequences of the poor diet available:

Worst of all, because of the poor food, and having only one kind of food without vegetables - and then that tinned beef - there came a sort of scurvy amongst the people. They got a sore mouth and a dreadful smell with it: in some cases the pallet fell out and the teeth, and some of the children were full of holes or sores in the mouth. And then they died...The mothers might never buy them anything; there were usually vegetables to be bought, but they might not go out of the camp, the head of the camp was strict...

Today...I am feeling somewhat better, but in the camp dying still goes on. Scarletina is raging there and daily several are being buried. In our country scarletina is not a dangerous sickness, often the children do not go to bed...they just lie down; but these poor children are so weak, not having had proper food for so long. The meat was miserable stuff... tinned beef once a week and once mutton.

In another extract from her writing, Mrs Badenhorst goes on to describe the feeling of utter misery and helplessness prevalent amongst the refugees, as new inmates are brought in by the British Army:

There was at this time no chance for us to hear anything from outside: we could see no telegrams and heard only that which we could not listen to with certainty; we only leaned bits here and there from women brought in by the columns, or from a convoy which brought in food. It was most miserable for me when the columns came in, for they always drove so many cattle before them and these, gathered in their hundreds and needing food and water, bellowed until the sound was heart-rending. I thought sometimes that I must fly to some place where I could not hear the sound of their misery, the neighing of the foals, the bleating of the sheep - it seemed in truth as if God's hand were to heavy upon us, both man and beast. Oh God dost Thou strive with us in Thine anger and chastise us in Thy wrath. Be merciful and wipe us not from the face of the earth.

The severe cold not only affected the camp inmates. In the severe winter of 1901, a major and his men and their six hundred mules who were caught without shelter near one of the camps were all found frozen to death. By January 1902, the death rate was running at 1800 per month, with the result that almost 28000 Boers and 13500 black Africans overall died in these concentration camps, the losses being mainly women and children, as the men were away fighting. Contrary to the expectations of the British, the high death rate of the women and children in the camps only served to heighten the Boers' determination to continue fighting rather than undermine their morale.

Nelus makes no mention in his diary of the burning of the farms or of the concentration camps, as he was more involved in the front-line fighting for most of his time in South Africa up to the battle of Paardeberg, after which he was invalided out to the military hospitals. He does however show considerable concern for

General Cronje's wife and the other women and children who had followed their husbands to the battlefield, and who had to lie low and still as the shells burst over their heads without knowing whether their husbands were alive or dead. He comments that "incidents like these will live when the main features of the war are ignored and forgotten." He would probably have said the same about the plight of the women in the concentration camps had he witnessed the terrible conditions they were kept under.

"Camp" in the winter of 1901

The Boer War, which was initially to have been "all over by Christmas", actually lasted for two years and nine months, and cost Britain dearly in money, bloodshed and horses. The army suffered over 100,000 casualties, with almost 22,000 killed, of which 5,774 died in the field where they fell from enemy action and 16,168 died subsequently from wounds received or from disease and poor medical care. 400,346 horses, mules and donkeys were also killed during the war. Over 7,000 Boers also lost their lives in action, plus the thousands mentioned above who died in the concentration camps set up by the British. The Boers and the Africaans filed compensation claims, and over £5 million was paid out by the British Government. Overall, it is estimated that the war cost the British tax-payer over £200 million, a vast sum even on today's values.

Spion Kop. The scene of one of the worst casualty figures of the War, when almost a whole regiment was killed. The trenches they had dug became their mass grave

Chapter Six

AFTER THE BOER WAR

On his return from South Africa in November 1900, Nelus entered a period of convalescence back at his parents' home alongside the canal in South Marston, where he used this spare time to prepare his diary for its publication in March 1901. Unfortunately, we do not know the nature of his illness, but it appears to be the recurrence of a previous complaint dating from before this war. It is possible that he contracted his complaint from his former overseas service in India, and it was sufficiently serious to get him released from active duty, although this was much against his wishes. Nevertheless, he kept himself busy whilst he was recovering by preparing his diary and on Friday, 15th February 1901, he gave a talk on his experiences in the Boer War at a concert in the village hall in South Marston, and this was reported in the local evening paper. He may well have been transferred to light duties with the army on his recovery, until his final transfer to the Army Reserve on 1st July 1902, when he received his war gratuity of £5. Whilst on Army Reserve, he found himself employment on the local farms as a labourer, and it was around this time that he renewed his acquaintance with his sweetheart - soon to become his future wife, Martha Anne Hunt, who was known to one and all as Annie.

Annie Hunt (Nelus' wife)

Annie's family had maintained a strong presence in South Marston and neighbouring villages such as Wroughton, Wootton Bassett and Highworth for many years, with the first mention in the parish records in South Marston church announcing the baptism of Hercules and William Hunt, sons of Thomas Hunt, on the 8th July 1609. Her family continues to appear regularly over the centuries, occasionally with the odd indiscretion, such as the entry in Marston's register for 13th September 1761, announcing the baptism of Mary, the "baseborn" daughter of Job Hunt and Frances Lock

Nelus Back home…and a visit from a colleague

A later member of the family of some local notoriety was "Granny Hunt" who also earned a mention in the works of Alfred Williams as follows:

At Wroughton, "Dicky" Austin, the old church clerk, nearly ninety years of age, lives in a small cottage halfway down the hill, together with a middle age daughter, who tends him in his infirmity......

........Dicky has many stories to tell, with many smiles, and a few tears coursing down his poor old cheeks, but it all seems so very long ago and no-one comes to talk with him about it and refresh his memory, especially since he has not been able to get out to see his old neighbour Granny Hunt who lives a stone's throw adown the hill.

Granny is aged ninety six; she would shame many a one at sixty. Her cottage door was wide open in the afternoon; she was busy scouring her candlesticks. 'I doos this every day o'mi life,' she declares. 'The candles as e gets nowadays tha do gutter so. 'Tis nothin so good as it used to be.' She is tallish and stoutish, stooping a little, though not much, with fine features, face deeply wrinkled, but with fresh, ruddy cheeks, robust and healthy looking; if outward indications are at all trustworthy, she should easily complete her centenary. Her cottage is small, consisting of one tiny room, and a pantry downstairs, and two small bedrooms above. The walls are pasted over with illustrated papers of sixty and seventy years ago, which give an antiquated air to the interior. Here and there are photographs of soldier and sailor sons, taken when the art was in its infancy, and one or two fine old coloured engravings. In her young days Granny did spinning and weaving, and also straw-platting, which were regular industries in the village; every cottage had a loom or a wheel in those days, enabling the poor folks to obtain a livelihood.

'Have you lived in the cottage long?' I asked.

'Lived yer, yes. Never lived nowhere else, as e knows on,' she answered. Then she went on to talk about her father who was carter, her husband who was carter, and her son who was carter, of feasting and revelling, back-swording, and leg-kicking, working for a penny a day in the fields, whipping-stocks, windmills, watermills, and other old-fashioned paraphernalia, until I felt to be whirled back a whole century, and to be lost to the present time altogether. By-and-by I found time to question her again.

'Do you enjoy good health?'

'Good 'ealth? Lar bless tha, no. E caant' walk no distance wi'out a stick, that e caant.'

'But have you never had any severe illness?' I ventured.

'Ye-es, severe illness, ye-es; but nothin' saarious, awhever,' she answered. 'My 'usband, look, 'e drapped down dead at the table yer, one Sunday a dinner-time. I was just gone in to the panterny, an' the vittals was on the table, an' I yerd a naize, an' I sed : 'Lar Willum, whatever be at? You bin an' knocked the leaf o' the table down'; but a niver answered ma, an' there a was crooched up dead, jest wher you be now, look.'

Annie's father (Jonah George Hunt)

Annie's father, Jonah George Hunt, like many others at that time, earned his living in the Great Western Railway Works in New Swindon, and lived in number 22 Exeter Street in the Town. This was part of the new model village built by the G.W.R to house their employees and families around the extensive new railway works it had brought to the area. The prestigious development made every effort to cater for all the needs of its workforce, not only with modern accommodation for all from management down, but also recreational facilities including theatre, swimming pool, library, churches and shops, all within walking distance of the place of work. There was never any excuse to be late for work as the start and finish times of all shifts were marked by a very loud hooter, which could be heard for miles around. This call became a familiar sound to all Swindonians, being used as a form of universal clock, doubling up as an air-raid siren during the Second World War, and even being sounded on the stroke of midnight on every new year's eve to welcome in the new year. The siren was mounted on the roof of the fitting and machine shop which was built in 1864, and had a range of approximately 12-15 miles. It was sounded every morning at 5.15, 5.45 and 6.00 and served its purpose well as it was impossible to ignore by anyone within its range. However, in 1868 the local lord of the manor, Lord Bolingbroke, at his mansion at nearby Lydiard Tregooze, was not amused at having his sleep disturbed at such an hour every morning, and a battle ensued when he tried to get it silenced. The working population of Swindon relied on their early morning call from the siren to ensure that they got to work on time and therefore did not lose valuable wages, and were not happy to dispense with this benefit in order that the lord could sleep in the mornings. The battle raged for six years, until Lord Bolingbroke finally got the hooter's license revoked in July 1874 for health reasons. The people of Swindon were not prepared to accept this decision, and by the new year they had managed to resurrect the custom with a new hooter, based on the argument that Lord Bolingbroke was only in residence at his mansion for two months of the year during the shooting season. The incident was commemorated in the Swindon Advertiser on 24th February 1873, by the following poem:

THE SWINDON HOOTER

Three miles away, as birds do fly
A grand Viscount resides
He owns three thousand acres
And many things besides.

A noble park, well stocked with game
A splendid mansion too
And Crusoe-like he's monarch of
All things that he can view.

Reposing on his bed of down
One fifteen-five in the morning
A fearful sound assailed his ears
Which set his Lordship storming.

Up from his couch, he rang the bell
John thought the house on fire
He rubbed his eyes and wondered what
Had roused his master's ire.

Away into his master's room
The footman quickly ran
In loud, severe and angry tones
The Viscount thus began.

"John, John, whence comes those fearful sounds
I shudder now to think on?"
Says John "Why that's the hooter, sir
They blow it at New Swindon.

They blow it every morning sir"
Says John ,"to wake the men"
"Oh blow the men," the Viscount said
Said John "It's off again."

Again his Lordship sought his couch
To rest his weary frame
And eer he just had forty winks
The hooter blew again.

"Flesh and blood cannot stand this"
So said the angry lord
"I'll write a sharpish letter to
The Swindon Local Board."

The Local Board, when next they met
Told him out straight and clear
That as 'twas for the public good
They should not interfere.

Said he, "I'll not be bothered
By any Local Boards
I'll quickly take the matter up
Before the House of Lords."

So let us join together, boys
And unity be showing
To do our best to keep our friend
The factory hooter blowing.

H.G.

Even though the railway works themselves have now gone, the bulk of the original model village remains, and forms the core of the modern town of new Swindon, leaving the old community of Old Swindon somewhat isolated on top of the hill. The hooter itself was finally silenced in 1986 when the old G.W.R Works eventually closed. At the time of writing, the old railway workshops have now been converted into a vast shopping centre, incorporating parts of the original buildings and machinery.

On Christmas Day, 1902, Nelus, now aged thirty, and Annie aged twenty three, were married in the parish church of St. Mary Magdalen, South Marston, the signing of the register being witnessed by Annie's sister Emily and her uncle, Edwin Warren. Although it seems strange to us today, a Christmas Day wedding was quite a common occurrence a hundred years ago, as "a day off" was a rare event, and if the nuptials could be arranged on a day when nobody was working anyway, then so much the better!

Nelus & Annie's wedding certificate

The arrangements would have been a slightly hurried affair, as Annie was already pregnant! In later life, she confided to her niece that on discovering her condition, she ran to her father and declared "you must let me get married or I will have to kill myself!" Fortunately, Jonah agreed! The vicar who performed the wedding ceremony was the same Angus Macdonald who regularly appears in the school records as actively taking part in its day to day running. The service, held on such a special day, conjures up the image of an idyllic romantic start to their marriage, and the scene is set with them taking their vows in the picturesque parish church, in front of their families and most of the villagers, all turned out in their Sunday best, in this rural little community on a frosty Christmas Morning. After the service, Christmas Lunch would have been served as the wedding breakfast, with the celebrations continuing well into the night on this extra special day.

We do not know where Nelus and Annie started off their married life together, but it would probably have been with one or other set of parents, most likely Nelus' at Canal Cottage, as being the youngest child, his siblings would have already flown the nest, leaving room for the young married couple. Annie, on the other hand, was from a larger family, having two brothers, Joe and Steve, and three sisters, Emily, Ellen and Ginny (otherwise known as Ada).

South Marston church where Nelus and Annie married on
Christmas Day 1901

Steve, (Annie's brother) as a young man and
in later life pictured with Annie

Joe spent some time in the army, and then married Gladys
Edgington and emigrated to Toronto, Canada, where they brought
up a family including twin boys. Ellen had a son called Abraham
who was born in South Marston in 1920, and later she married a
Mr Kent who lived in Old Town Swindon. Steve married, and had
two daughters Margaret and Hilda, who are still living in the area

today. Ginny married a Mr Farr who already had a daughter named Edie.

Annie's sisters Nellie and Ginny taken in 1931

Emily was the only one who never married, although she had a sweetheart in the Navy called Ernest Cole. In later life, she too emigrated to Canada where she spent the rest of her life. Like most young girls of the period, all four sisters were in service for a while, and were able to keep each other informed of suitable positions arising around the area. Their mother died when Steve, the eldest boy, was aged nine, and their father Jonah later remarried. Ada moved in with him in the family home in Exeter Street, Swindon to care for him during his final years.

Previous page shows Annie's sisters Emily (front left) and Nellie (front right) as bridesmaids at their brother Joe's wedding. Nelus' half-sister Olive and her husband Fred are on the far left.

Sunday 16th August 1903 saw Nelus and Annie back in the village church for the christening of their son Aubrey Leslie Cornelius Head, who was to be their only child. Shortly after this the family moved to Omdurman Street in New Swindon, and it is likely that Nelus resumed his employment in the Great Western Railway Works that he had originally left when he first joined the army in 1891. Army life, however, had made Nelus restless, and from then on he could not seem to hold down a job for very long. Perhaps it was having been on active service in foreign parts for nearly ten years that made an ordinary civilian job seem too mundane to him, for he seemed in constant search of a little more excitement in his life. Between their wedding in 1902 and his enlistment back into the army in the Great War on 26th September 1914, a period of less than twelve years, they had some fifteen different addresses, as they moved around the area taking up new positions of employment. Most of these were at farms and estates around the Swindon area, including the Bolingbroke Estate mentioned previously, and racing stables in Lambourn, filling the positions of housekeeper and gardener/handyman. Nelus even did a short spell of strawberry-picking in France. Despite these frequent moves, their work was still highly regarded, as several surviving references show, including the one from Lambourn shown overleaf.

In October 1909 the family moved into one of the four farm cottages on Roves Farm in the village of Sevenhampton, just across the fields from South Marston, where the school records show that their son Aubrey was admitted to the village school on 14th October.

Roves Farm is now a thriving tourist attraction as a working farm open to the public, especially popular in the lambing season. The pair of cottages where they lived remain today, but are now converted to an attractive single dwelling.

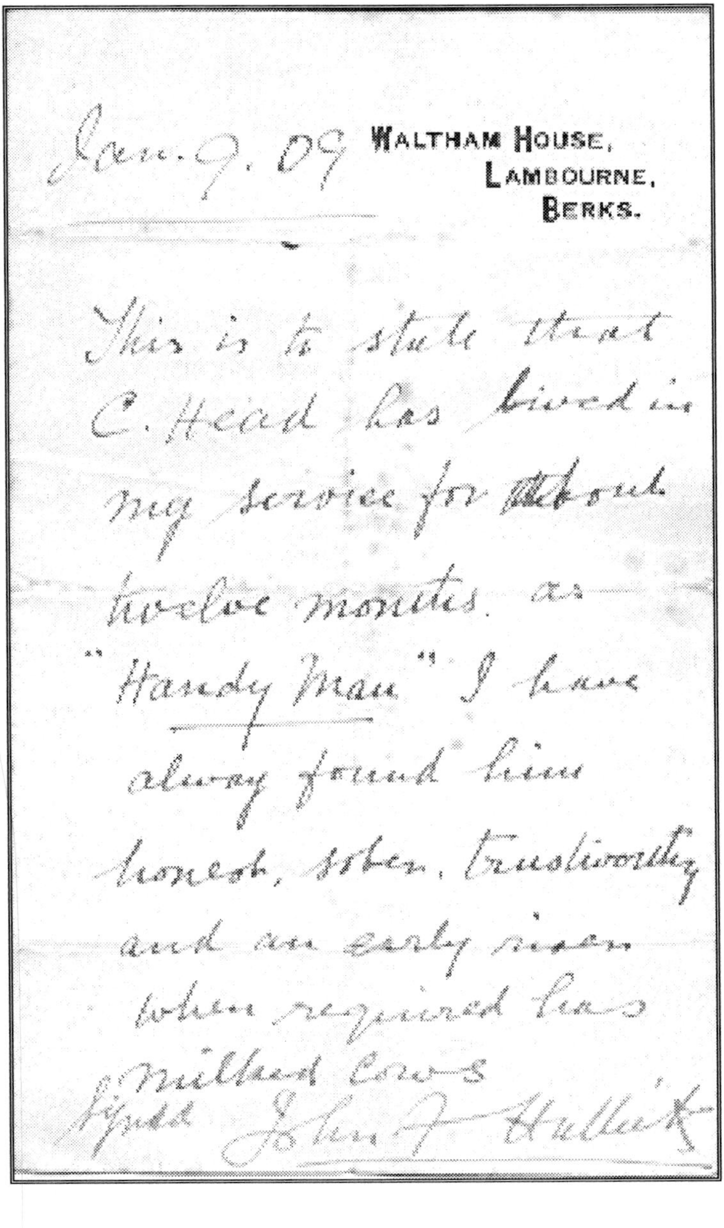

Jan. 9. 09   WALTHAM HOUSE,
                       LAMBOURNE,
                            BERKS.

This is to state that
C. Head has lived in
my service for about
twelve months. as
"Handy Man" I have
always found him
honest, sober, trustworthy
and an early riser.
when required has
milked cows
Signed John J. Hallett

199

Nelus, Annie and their son Aubrey at Roves Farm

Pony and trap from Roves Farm

Three years later, they moved back to South Marston when Nelus took up employment at Manor Farm. For the next two years they lived in Exstone Cottage in the centre of the village; one of the newly-built "Bell" cottages owned by the Manor. Today, the cottage, although extended, still has the same general appearance, and looks down the lane towards the church where Nelus and Annie were married. In 1914, two more moves followed in quick succession to racing stables in Wantage and Great Shefford in Berkshire, where Annie was housekeeper for the stable lads, and Nelus held the post of handyman. During this time they started what was to become a life-long friendship with the champion jockey Sir Gordon Richards.

Gordon Richards as a young man

It was from here on 26th September that Nelus enlisted into the Military Foot Police at the age of 42, while Annie stayed on in service for a while in the racing stables.

Nelus in his Military Foot Police uniform

The Military Foot Police only recruited men with at least four years service from other branches of the army. Only men of good character and with one good conduct badge were accepted, and all were transferred in at the rank of lance-corporal, as there were no privates in the Corps. They were stationed in garrison towns at home and abroad, and their main purpose was to maintain order amongst the soldiers, with their importance being highest while on active service. Sometimes, however, things did not go quite according to plan. In January 1916, after the withdrawal from Gallipoli, confusion reigned on the beaches where piles of stores had been abandoned by the retreating troops, and the Military Police had been set to guard these dumps. These orders were overruled, and the troops were allowed to loot the goods, resulting in them arriving at the evacuation boats laden down with all manner of useless goods, and large numbers of bottles of alcohol, with the obvious outcome. The Military Police were sent to smash the bottles, and the alcohol fumes released had the surprise result of intoxicating the Military Policemen, many of whom were teetotalers, much to the delight of the Officer in Command.

Nelus would have been very sought after by the Military Police due to his army experience in both India and South Africa. Unfortunately, as most of the military records were destroyed during the Second World War, we do not know much about his movements during this period; however, from correspondence, it appears that he served the first eighteen months following his re-enlistment in England waiting for a posting abroad, and on a postcard he sent home to Annie from Aldershot, dated 12th May 1916, he states "no news about going out yet." Two weeks later he was posted overseas with the British Expeditionary Force, and an entry in his "Active Service" Testament Book says:

Number 232P
Lance Cpl. C.Head
Mil F Police
The Docks
Marsailles
Dated 24.6.16.

On the opposite page to this entry is a handwritten message to the troops from General, Lord Roberts, the mainstay commander of the Boer War, whom Nelus had served under in South Africa, and who was a popular, well-respected figure with his men. It reads as follows:

LORD ROBERTS MESSAGE TO THE TROOPS

25th August 1914

I wish you to put your trust in God. He will watch over you and strengthen you. You will find in this little Book guidance when you are in health, comfort when you are in sickness, and strength when you are in adversity.

<u>Roberts</u>

Members of the B.E.F. on their way to the Front

From postcards sent home, it appears that Nelus had been involved in the Battle of the Somme, although he was one of the fortunate ones to survive the awful carnage. On 10th August 1917 his service with the B.E.F. ended, either due to sickness or injury in France, and he then returned home to England. A postcard from him to Annie tells us that he had arrived at Southampton, and was being transferred by ambulance train to the London District Hospital. This card was written in haste, and carried the message "I am fairly well." This ambulance train could well have been one built by the Great Western Railway Company at Swindon as their part of the war effort. Each train was made up of nine coaches, two for doctors, nurses and orderlies, five as mobile wards, a dining car and finally a pharmacy car with operating room and dispensary. Ninety eight patients could be accommodated together with twelve staff.

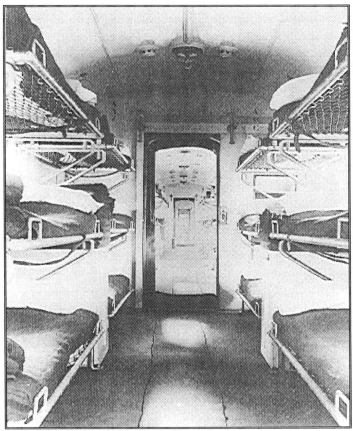
Interior of a hospital train

The interiors were painted white, and lit by gas, with ample water storage and steam heating apparatus, and a gangway left wide enough to move a patient on a stretcher into the operating room from any part of the train. A large red cross on a white background was emblazoned on the side and roof of every coach. When the first two trains had been built in Swindon, interest was such that there was a queue, four deep, which continued for four hours at

the Railway Works, as the public came to view these trains at a fee
of 6d each (donated to the Red Cross Society).

Selection of postcards Nelus sent home from the Great War

Although Nelus illness or injury was serious enough for him to be
brought back from the front, by the 29th August he had already
rejoined his unit at Aldershot, and on the 17th September he was
ordered to proceed to Relford, Nottinghamshire, where he
presumably remained until the 12th November when he was
transferred to the Labour Corps (now the Pioneer Corps) as a
private. On 25th November he was posted to 298 Reserve Labour

Company, and again appointed Lance Corporal, a rank he lost within weeks as he was deprived of his stripe by the Commanding Officer on Boxing Day, 1917. Losing one's stripe was a fairly common punishment issued for such minor offences as drunkeness or insubordination; we wonder what his reason was - perhaps the strain of yet another war and active service had been just too much!

Nelus, (far left, top) with comrades at the barracks

Due to the long periods of separation between Nelus and Annie during this war, they started to write poetry to each other, and at Christmas 1917, Annie sent him the following poem on the back of the postcard illustrated:

YOUR KING AND COUNTRY THANK YOU
OH LOYAL SOULS AND STRONG
WHO SIDE BY SIDE
AND STEADFAST EYED
STOOD FAST TO RIGHT THE WRONG.
WHO LEFT YOUR HOME BEHIND YOU
AND TOOK ON SHOULDERS FREE
THE STRONG MAN'S YOKE;
THAT WEAKER FOLK;
SECURE FROM HARM SHOULD BE.
WHO BRAVED FOR THEM THE PERIL
FOR THEM THE HARDER LINE

THROUGH SUMMER'S GLOW
AND WINTER'S SNOW
THESE THREE LONG YEARS OF WAR
GREAT HOSTS WHERE ALL ARE HEROES
CAN E'RE WE PAY OUR DEBT?
YOUR KING AND COUNTRY THANKYOU
AND NEVER WILL FORGET!

Annie's postcard

As by this time homesickness was beginning to take its toll, with Nelus being away at war for so long, letters from home were welcomed all the more, and he wrote the following verse back to Annie in response to her card, as no doubt tens of thousands of other serving men wrote in the same vein to their sweethearts back home:

WRITE TO ME VERY OFTEN
WRITE TO ME VERY SOON
LETTERS TO ME ARE DEAREST
THAN THE LOVELIEST FLOWERS IN JUNE

THEY ARE THE AFFECTION TORCHES
THE LIGHTING OF FRIENDSHIP LAMP
FLITTERING AROUND THE HEARTSTRING
LIKE FIREFLIES IN THE CAMP

WRITE TO ME VERY OFTEN
WRITE TO ME IN THE EARLY MORN
OR AT THE CLOSE OF EVENING
WHEN THE WHOLE DAY IS GONE

DRAW UP THAT LITTLE TABLE CLOSE
TO THE FIRE AND WRITE
WRITE TO ME IN THE MORNING
OR WRITE TO ME AT NIGHT

WRITE TO ME VERY OFTEN
LETTERS ARE LINKS THAT BIND
THRUTHFUL HEARTS TO EACH OTHER
FLITTERING MIND TO MIND

GIVING TO KINDRED SPIRITS
LASTING AND TRUE DELIGHT
IF YOU WOULD STRENGTHEN FRIENDSHIP
NEVER FORGET TO WRITE

Nelus was posted again to the 304 Reserve Labour Company at the beginning of March 1918, and was finally discharged from the army six and a half weeks later, on the 20th May 1918, nearly 27 years after first enlisting, and after serving three years and eight months in the Great War. According to his record, he was discharged as no longer physically fit for war service. At about the same time that he was leaving the army, his son Aubrey was enlisting for a career in the Navy, and finally ended up as an electrician in civilian life.

Aubrey in Naval uniform

Whilst Nelus was away at war, Annie moved from the racing stables in Berkshire into 27 Eastcott Road, Old Town, Swindon, which she rented from a local landlord, and which they later purchased from him on a private mortgage, a common practice in those days. They continued paying on a weekly basis, but as mortgage repayment instead of rent. To purchase rather than rent a house was not as usual or easy as it is today, and Nelus and Annie were obviously overjoyed at this new-found property ownership, and treated themselves to a "78" recording of "My Aine Wee House", which we later found in the chest. This house was an end-of-terrace, two-bedroomed property built around the turn of the century, and was to be their home for the rest of their lives. It is situated on the brow of Eastcott Hill which runs between Old and New Swindon, and at the time of their occupation, would not have possessed such luxuries as a bathroom or hot running water; the sole facilities being an outside privy sited in the garden, consisting of a small shed furnished with a wooden plank with two large circular holes. "Double-seaters" were often found in Wiltshire; perhaps our forebears were more sociable in such matters than we are today!

The house in Eastcott Hill

The ground floor of the house consisted of a hall, a small front room (only to be used on special occasions and containing Nelus' acquisitions from his travels abroad), a living room and scullery at the back. The accommodation most probably would have seemed a little cramped compared with the village properties that they had rented, but at least it was their own, and they had the benefit of running water rather than the tiresome task of drawing from the well. Even so, they still found room for an old aunt, Elizabeth Bridges (nee Lewis), also from the village of South Marston, who lived with them until her death in 1925 at the age of ninety. The bill for her funeral amounted to £9.12s.6d, and still survives. A frequent visitor to this house was the famous champion jockey, Sir Gordon Richards, who had known Annie from her racing stable days, and maintained a life-long friendship, often staying with them when he was in the area.

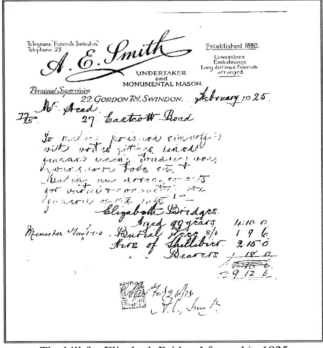

The bill for Elizabeth Bridges' funeral in 1925

A short walk away was the commercial centre of the Old Town, and it was here that Nelus was employed for three years as the gardener at the Kings Arms Hotel in Wood Street, an inn dating from the 1830's, which was rebuilt in 1870 and still retains the same appearance today, except that the hotel garden he once lovingly tended is now lost under a modern car park. It is sad to think that all his hard work was sacrificed to the needs of the motor car.

Wood Street where Nelus worked (halfway up on left)

Prior to this he had worked for a Captain Buchan at 78 Goddard Avenue, a five minute walk away from their house, who, according to his reference, found him "a most trustworthy and obliging, capable and conscientious worker" during the three years he was employed by him, "being most clean and thorough in all his work."

Goddard Avenue was, at that time, a highly respectable tree-lined road of gentlemen's residences, and was occupied by some of the wealthier professional classes, many of whom would have employed staff for the general day-to-day running of the house and garden. At number 132 lived Alderman Reuben George, mayor of Swindon, and a well-known and much respected local character, who, in 1931, also provided Nelus and Annie with a glowing reference when they applied for a local position as school caretaker.

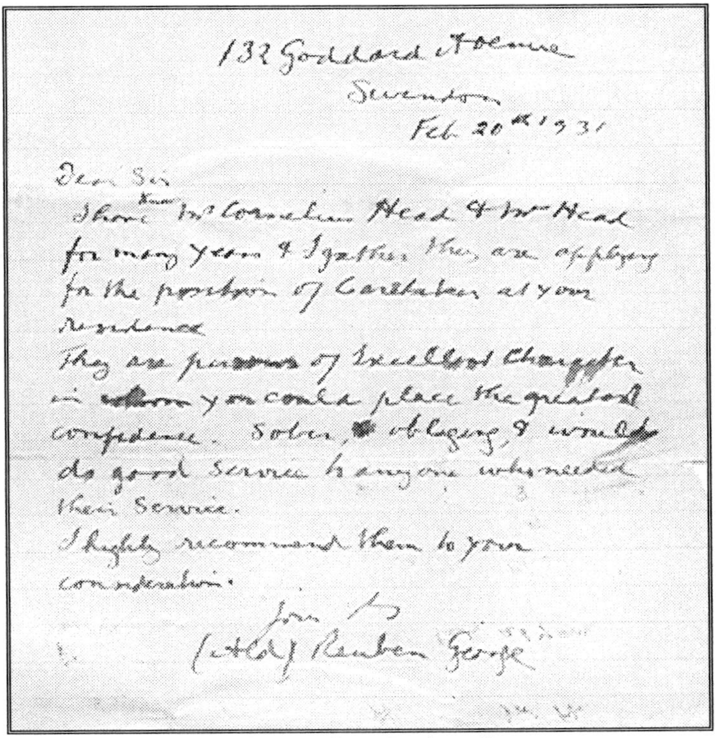

132 Goddard Avenue
Swindon
Feb 20th 1931

Dear Sir
I have [known] Mr Cornelius Head & Mrs Head
for many years & I gather they are applying
for the position of Caretakers at your
residence
They are persons of excellent character
in whom you could place the greatest
confidence. Sober, obliging & would
do good service to anyone who needed
their service.
I highly recommend them to your
consideration.

Yours [truly]
[sgd] Reuben George

The reference from Reuben George

This new job would not have lasted very long, as on the 19th May 1934 Nelus died from cancer of the bladder, at the Victoria Hospital in Old Town, Swindon, with Annie at his bedside. He was 62 years old.

Although Nelus had served in two major wars as well as the actions in India, Annie still had to fight to get a war widows' pension.

Annie survived for a further 31 years, living in the same house until her death on 28th February 1965, in her 85th year. Aubrey, their son, by then himself widowed, was living with her, and he discovered her collapsed from a heart attack on the bedroom floor that morning.

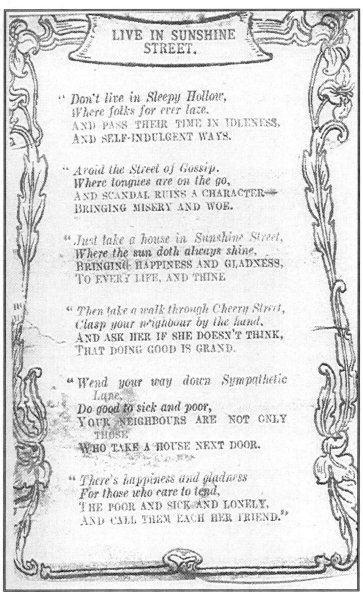

LIVE IN SUNSHINE STREET.

" *Don't live in Sleepy Hollow,*
  Where folks for ever laze.
  AND PASS THEIR TIME IN IDLENESS,
  AND SELF-INDULGENT WAYS.

" *Avoid the Street of Gossip.*
  Where tongues are on the go,
  AND SCANDAL RUINS A CHARACTER—
  BRINGING MISERY AND WOE.

" *Just take a house in Sunshine Street,*
  Where the sun doth always shine,
  BRINGING HAPPINESS AND GLADNESS,
  TO EVERY LIFE, AND THINE

" *Then take a walk through Cheery Street,*
  Clasp your neighbour by the hand,
  AND ASK HER IF SHE DOESN'T THINK,
  THAT DOING GOOD IS GRAND.

" *Wend your way down Sympathetic*
  Lane,
  Do good to sick and poor,
  YOUR NEIGHBOURS ARE NOT ONLY
  THOSE
  WHO TAKE A HOUSE NEXT DOOR.

" *There's happiness and gladness*
  For those who care to tend,
  THE POOR AND SICK AND LONELY,
  AND CALL THEM EACH HER FRIEND."

Nelus and Annie's philosophy for life - found in Nelus' chest

A few years later, he too suffered a heart attack, and was found dead in the house.

Jazzer the dog when young with Nelus, and as an old dog
keeping the widowed Annie company

MINISTRY OF DEFENCE CS(RM)2b
Bourne Avenue Hayes Middlesex UB3 1RF

Telephone 0181-573 3831 ext   318

Your reference

Our reference
96/22704/CS(RM)2B/4
Date
2 June 1996

Dear Ms Morris

In reply to your letter dated 1 February 1996, please accept our apologies for the delay Our records show the following particulars of the military service of **500062 (formerly 232 and 3709) Private Corneilieus HEAD - Labour Corps.**

Enlisted into the Oxfordshire Light Infantry on a Short Service Engagement and posted
to Depot	22.09.1891
Posted to 1st Battalion	01.01.1892
Passed 3rd Class Certificate of Education	16.04.1892
Posted to the 2nd Battalion	04.02.1893
Passed 2nd Class Certificate of Education	06.03.1894
Transferred to the Army Reserve in India	01.12.1898
Discharged from the Reserve	03.12.1899
Rejoined the Colours and posted to Details	04.12.1899
Re-transferred to Army Reserve	01.07.1902
Paid War Gratuity of £5.00	Date not recorded
Re-engaged for 4 years on reserve	19.09.1903
Discharged on termination of Engagement	21.09.1907
Enlisted into the Military Police Depot and appointed Lance Corporal	26.09.1914
Transferred to the Labour Corps as a Private	12.11.1917
Posted to 298 Reserve Labour Company	25.11.1917
Appointed Lance Corporal	Date not recorded
Deprived of Lance Stripe by Commanding Officer	26.12.1917
Posted to 304 Reserve Labour Company	03.03.1918
Discharged	20.05.1918

Cause of Discharge: No longer physically fit for war service

Service with the Colours: 22.09.1891 - 30.11.1898 and 04.12.1899 - 30.06.1902 and
  26.09.1914 - 20.05.1918

Overseas Service:	India	04.02.1893 - 31.11.1898 and 04.12.1899 - 21.12.1899
	South Africa	22.12.1899 - 20.10.1900
	British Expeditionary Force	26.05.1916 - 10.08.1917

Medals issued etc: Queens South Africa Medal with Clasps Paardeberg and Relief of Kimberley.

Other information extracted from the file which may be of interest is as follows:

Place of Birth: South Marston, Swindon, Wiltshire
Apparent age on 1st enlistment: 19 years 5 months
Height: 5ft 9¼"
Chest measurement: Minimum 35 inches
                     Maximum 37 inches
Complexion: Fair
Eyes: Brown
Hair: Light Brown
Weight: 146lbs

Next of kin: Ephraim and Anne Head (father and mother) South Marston, Swindon, Wiltshire

Trade on 1st Enlistment: Labourer

There is one brother Arthur recorded. The above named married Martha Anne Flint on 25.12.1902 at
South Marston Wiltshire. A son Aubrey Leslie was born 21.09.1903.

Personal details for 2nd Enlistment:

Height: 5ft 9¾ins
Weight: 168lbs
Girth when fully expanded: 37ins
Range of expansion: 2½ins
Trade on enlistment: Cook
Apparent age: 46 years 2 months

Next of kin: Mrs Martha Anne Head (wife) Great Stafford, Berkshire

I hope the above information proves both helpful and interesting.

                         Yours sincerely

                         M J Parke

                         M J PARKE (Mrs)
                         for Departmental Record Officer

GJ